The Proper Care of
TURTLES

Albino Desert Tortoise, *Gopherus agassizii*. Photo by Alex Kerstitch.

Facing page: A rare and fascinating sight: a young two-headed example of the Midland Painted Turtle, *Chrysemys picta marginata*. Photo by Jeff Wines.

1995 Edition

Distributed in the UNITED STATES to the Pet Trade by T.F.H. Publications, Inc., One T.F.H. Plaza, Neptune City, NJ 07753; distributed in the UNITED STATES to the Bookstore and Library Trade by National Book Network, Inc. 4720 Boston Way, Lanham MD 20706; in CANADA to the Pet Trade by H & L Pet Supplies Inc., 27 Kingston Crescent, Kitchener, Ontario N2B 2T6; Rolf C. Hagen Ltd., 3225 Sartelon Street, Montreal 382 Quebec; in CANADA to the Book Trade by Vanwell Publishing Ltd., 1 Northrup Crescent, St. Catharines, Ontario L2M 6P5 ; in ENGLAND by T.F.H. Publications, PO Box 15, Waterlooville PO7 6BQ; in AUSTRALIA AND THE SOUTH PACIFIC by T.F.H. (Australia), Pty. Ltd., Box 149, Brookvale 2100 N.S.W., Australia; in NEW ZEALAND by Brooklands Aquarium Ltd. 5 McGiven Drive, New Plymouth, RD1 New Zealand; in Japan by T.F.H. Publications, Japan—Jiro Tsuda, 10-12-3 Ohjidai, Sakura, Chiba 285, Japan; in SOUTH AFRICA by Lopis (Pty) Ltd., P.O. Box 39127, Booysens, 2016, Johannesburg, South Africa. Published by T.F.H. Publications, Inc.
MANUFACTURED IN THE UNITED STATES OF AMERICA
BY T.F.H. PUBLICATIONS, INC.

The Proper Care of
TURTLES

JOHN COBORN

DEDICATION

This book is for my good friend Prof. Dr. sc. med. Walter Kirsche, who transformed a goodly portion of his back yard near Berlin, northern Germany, into a haven for Mediterranean tortoises!

The Chinese Redneck Turtle, *Chinemys kwangtungensis,* was only described in the mid-30's by North American herpetologist Clifford Pope. Photo by R. D. Bartlett.

CONTENTS

Author's Preface. 7

Evolution and Classification 16

Some Turtle Biology 31

Housing Your Turtles 39

Foods and Feeding 65

Hygiene and General Care 78

Reproduction and Captive
          Propagation 109

A Selection of Species 129

Bibliography 253

Index

Author's Preface

Turtles are familiar to all of us, and in spite of the fact that they are reptiles, they are viewed by the majority of people with a greater benevolence than would ever be applied to crocodiles or snakes.

Over the centuries turtles have indeed influenced and entertained many branches of mankind. In mythology there are numerous tales of how turtles have affected the lives of many races of people. An ancient Hindu belief was that the whole earth was supported on the backs of four elephants, who in turn stood on the carapace of an immense

Facing page: Tortoises have been kept as pets for centuries and today their popularity is still very strong. Photo of the Radiated Tortoise, *Geochelone radiata*, by R. D. Bartlett.

turtle swimming in an eternal sea. Ancient Chinese myths include the fact that the divine tortoise Kwei spent 18,000 years creating the universe and manufacturing the earth, moon, sun, and stars. In Japanese legends turtles are regarded as symbols of peace, good fortune, and success. One of these Japanese legends tells the story of a couple that was so deeply in love that they became immortal and remained youthful lovers for three hundred years. Eventually the spell was broken and the man turned into a turtle; the woman, a crane. The two creations henceforth living together as demigods. The Japanese also appreciate turtles as items of art, and there are many fine collectible pieces of carved ivory or jade depicting

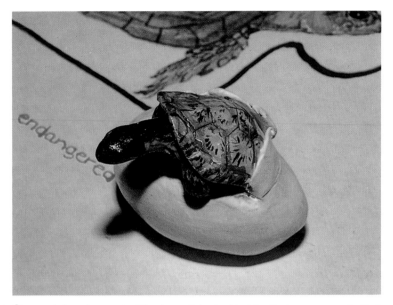

One peripheral aspect of the herpetological hobby that many people find fascinating involves the many avenues of artwork. Shown here is a porcelain sculpture of a hatching Bog Turtle, *Clemmys muhlenbergii.* Photo by W. P. Mara.

forms of these reptiles.

The ancient Greeks also showed interest in turtles. There are many illustrations and references to them in early Greek literature. Statues and toy replicas of tortoises were made by many early Mediterranean civilizations. The Romans even used the word "testudo" as a military term. Testudo, a word used today to denote a particular family of tortoises, Testudinidae, plus a genus therein, *Testudo,* was the original Latin name for tortoise, and a formation of troops besieging a fortress, protecting their heads with shields, was also termed a testudo. Another, more sinister, use of the word was for lute or lyre; a reference perhaps to the use of tortoise shells in the construction of such musical instruments.

In Papua New Guinea, a native tribe of the mountains believes that the thigh bone of a river turtle (probably *Carettochelys insculpta*, found only in the coastal areas many miles away from their remote villages) will soothe pain and heal wounds. High prices may be paid for such a bone.

The Amerindian tribes

The Chinese Stripe-necked Turtle, *Ocadia sinensis*, belongs to a genus that is considered one of the most primitive in the family Emydidae. Photo by R. D. Bartlett.

almost all have their own turtle legends, the best known of which is possibly the North American Indian story of the Great Turtle and the Little Turtle.

sky. The Great Turtle asked the Little Turtle to ascend into the heavens in order to produce light. Using a cloud as transportation, she thus traveled about the

A beautiful post-hatching example of *Notochelys platynota*. Some consider this turtle to be a close relative of those in the genus *Cyclemys*. Photo by R. D. Bartlett.

Though the story varies from tribe to tribe, the crux of the tale is that the earth was supported on the back of the Great Turtle but there was no light in the

firmament collecting together bolts of lightning that she rolled up into a large bright ball, and a small, less bright ball—the sun and the moon

Captive breeding is undoubtedly one of the most exciting aspects of turtle husbandry. Photo of a neonatal (just born) Radiated Tortoise, *Geochelone radiata*, by R. D. Bartlett.

respectively. The burrowing animals were then asked to make holes in the corners of the sky so that the sun and moon could enter and exit, thereby creating the day and the night.

There are many other myths and legends about turtles, far too many to mention here of course, but a study of them is an interesting sideline. Other peripheral aspects of the turtle fancy include the collection of turtle statues and ornaments, turtle pictures, and turtle postage stamps (many countries have produced postage stamps depicting turtles. It is very interesting and sometimes even profitable). Turtle photography can also be quite a rewarding pastime.

The major subject of this volume, however, is the proper care of turtles in captivity. For many years turtles of various kinds have been kept as pets, many species being available in the local pet shops. Unfortunately though, some were not quite as easy to keep as many people imagined, and in the earlier years of turtle keeping, tens of thousands of them perished due to lack of husbandry knowledge on the part of the keeper. Indeed, collecting for the pet trade in some countries has led to a serious decline in wild populations and brought some species to the brink of extinction.

Land tortoises from sunny southern Europe and North Africa, for example, were once collected on an enormous scale and taken by container truck to chilly northern cities and sold as pets. Most of these never survived their first winter, as the trauma of the journey and the resulting stress of an alien climate never allowed them to feed up enough reserves to get them through a relatively long period of northern hibernation. Luckily,

The Red-eared Slider, *Pseudemys scripta elegans*, is very likely the most commonly kept aquatic turtle of all time. Photo by Dr. Herbert R. Axelrod.

various conservation bodies saw the dangers of over-collection and lobbied for legal protection of many species. This eventually resulted in international controls with regard to the collection, export, and import of many species.

Fortunately, many

species of turtle are still available for the enthusiast. Recent intensive study of the habitats and behavior of the reptiles has led to a greater understanding of their captive requirements, such that pet turtles can live long and happy lives and probably even breed. Indeed, the main aim of all turtle keepers should be to encourage their pets to reproduce and thus help relieve burdens on wild populations. Every captive-bred specimen supplied to a turtle enthusiast will be one less collected from the wild!

Historically, people have always kept pets of one form or another, but in recent years the demand for more unusual pets has seen a marked increase. The reason for this is probably because the ever-evolving urban man subconsciously likes to keep a symbol of nature and the great outdoors. While turtle enthusiasts may not be as numerous as fish fanatics or bird fanciers, they certainly make up for this with enthusiasm for their chosen subject. I have been a "cheloniaphile" for many years and have kept several species, both professionally as a reptile curator and privately for my own pleasure. This book is meant to give inspiration and information to all grades of turtle enthusiast and provide a guide to the proper care of these charming creatures in captivity. To do this it is necessary to give details of the species' wild habitats. While I have personally had the good fortune to visit the natural habitats of many species and have successfully kept many more, I have, of course, had to draw on the literature in order to supplement my own experiences. A short list of items for further reading is given in the bibliography at the end of the text.

Many hobbyists prefer to start with very young turtles, like this small Eastern Painted Turtle, *Chrysemys picta picta*, and raise them into adulthood. Photo by W. P. Mara.

At this stage I would like to express my sincere appreciation of the patience and dedication of the editorial staff of TFH publications who, without protest, have had to endure the trials and tribulations of many of my manuscripts over the years. It is always truly amazing for me to see my pile of patiently typed, dog-eared manuscript pages miraculously transformed into a colorfully illustrated volume. To use an Australian expression: "good on ya mates" and keep up the good work!

John Coborn
Nanango, Queensland

Evolution and Classification

The main objective of this book is to deal with the proper care of living turtles and tortoises, those contemporary members of the reptilian order Chelonia, which can be conveniently described collectively as "chelonians." Every hobbyist, however, likes to know more about the background of his chosen subject, so let us start at the beginning of the turtle story and contemplate briefly the origins of our shelled friends.

To be very brief, it is generally accepted that single-celled life began in the water, and over millions of years it evolved into a more complex form. Eventually the first vertebrate animals arrived, these being numerous species of fish that swarmed in the seas, lakes, and rivers. As the earth's surface was still in various degrees of volcanic and meteorological turmoil, some of these fish had to gradually develop more sophisticated ways of dealing with the frequent changes in water quantity and quality. Over great periods of time, some developed lungs. From these, the first amphibians evolved. They breathed with lungs instead of gills and were thus able to utilize atmospheric oxygen, and since they had limbs rather than fins, they were able to move about on land though they still had to find water in order to reproduce. To successfully deal with further water shortages, certain amphibians began

It is generally accepted that the amphibians evolved long before the reptiles did. Turtles did not appear until the Triassic Period, about 240 million years ago. Photo of *Chelydra serpentina osceola* by Michael Cardwell.

to develop more efficient means of living on land, and these included reproducing out of the water.

To successfully live and reproduce in the gaseous atmosphere, several further adaptations were required. The most important of these adaptations were: a skin that was relatively impermeable to moisture which helped prevent loss of body fluids; a means of internal fertilization; and a tough-shelled egg which could withstand the rigors of atmospheric weather as well as conserve moisture. The first vertebrates to develop these important qualities were the cotylosaurs or, early reptiles. More advanced reptiles became virtually the rulers of the land and remained so for millions of years. During this period many kinds of reptiles came and went, including the well-known dinosaurs which were the dominant animals of the earth for millions of years before they finally became extinct. The order Chelonia appeared relatively early on in reptile history, even earlier than the dinosaurs, making turtles a very old group that has remained relatively unchanged since the mid-Triassic Period some 200 million years ago.

Chelonians are thought to be direct descendants of the cotylosaurs, a possible connection being a small reptile fossil from the Permian (250-260 million years ago) beds of South Africa. Described as Eunotosaurus, this creature would superficially have resembled a small, plump lizard. However, the fossil shows a limited number of vertebrae and ribs so broadly expanded that they touched each other. Though there is no definite proof that this was a turtle ancestor, the anatomy surely shows some convincing clues, the vertebral and rib adaptations possibly being an early manifestation of the chelonian shell.

As far as we can tell from fossil records, the first of the true chelonians appeared in the mid or late Triassic period by which

Facing page: Although virtually impossible to maintain as pets, sea turtles are nevertheless fascinating, graceful creatures. Photo of the Hawksbill Turtle by Dr. Herbert R. Axelrod.

time they already had most of the typical characteristics of our modern turtles. The chelonian shell, of course, was developed as an armor for protection against the existed from the late Triassic to the Pleistocene periods. Before becoming extinct, however, the Amphichelydia formed the basis from which the modern suborders of

The Wood Turtle, *Clemmys insculpta*, gets its species name from the sculptured appearance of its carapace. Photo by Dr. Warren E. Burgess.

numerous carnivorous reptiles that abounded at the time, and over the years it seems to have served its purpose very well indeed. The first known turtles formed a suborder, Amphichelydia, which turtles, the Cryptodira and the Pleurodira, emerged.

The Amphichelydia contained the family Triassochelidae of which two genera, *Triassochelys* and *Proganochelys* are fairly well-represented by fossil evidence. *Proganochelys*, for example, differed from its immediate ancestors by having the bones of the skull reduced in number, teeth absent from the turtle evolution since the Triassic. Modern turtles are completely toothless, while the more advanced forms have developed the ability to withdraw the head,

Among the most specialized turtles are those in the family Trionychidae, known in the hobby as the "softshells." Photo by G. Dingerkus.

margins of the jaws, and the body protected by a robust shell. These basic turtle adaptations have been further refined during limbs, and tail completely within the shell, an action which *Proganochelys* was apparently unable to perform.

CLASSIFICATION OF THE CHELONIA

Until the latter half of the 18th century, scientists had great difficulty in categorizing the ever-increasing number of types of flora and fauna being collected from all corners of the earth. It was Swedish biologist Karl von Linne (generally known as Linnaeus) who revolutionized the naming and classification of living things by inventing what he called his "binomial system." In this system, each species was given a double scientific name, usually derived from the Latin, a language which was universally used by scientists at the time, although other languages or names may have been used from time to time. For example, the first European land tortoise was described by Linnaeus in 1758 as *Testudo graeca*. The first name, *Testudo* (which, appropriately, is Latin for tortoise), is that of the genus. The second name, *graeca*, is the specific name which means Greek. While there may be several species in a genus (*Testudo hermanni*, *Testudo marginata*, for example), there is only one species *Testudo graeca*. Species are normally at the bottom of the hierarchical scale and are characterized as animals which are basically the same morphologically and physiologically, and which, perhaps even more importantly, can naturally produce fertile offspring.

During Linnaeus' time, the science of zoology was still in its infancy and internationally inconsistent. Although many animals had common names, these names differed from language to language and even from dialect to dialect. Additionally, animals had not been studied in depth and the different groups were not adequately distinguished from each

The word "testudo" is Latin for tortoise, and there are currently five accepted species in the genus of the same name. Photo of *Testudo hermanni* by A. Jesse.

other. With generally accepted and internationally understood Latin names however, a zoologist could, and still can, understand what species is being referred to and to which category it belongs, whatever his own native language happens to be. *Testudo graeca*, for example, is known as the

Mediterranean or Greek Tortoise in English, Maurische Landschildkroete (Moorish Land- armored- toad) in German, Tortue Mauresque (Tortoise Moorish) in French and Testuggine Greca (Tortoise Greek) in Italian. In Russian it is something like Sredezemnawrskaya Cherepaha, but please don't ask me what the literal translation of this is!

As we have seen, there may be one or more species in a genus. Genera (plural of genus) are grouped together by similarities into families, families into orders and suborders, orders into classes and so on. Thus our *Testudo graeca* is placed with other members of the genus *Testudo* into the family Testudinidae, which contains about 15 other genera with similarities (examples include *Chelonoidis*, *Chersina*, *Gopherus*, and so on).

The hierarchical system may be more simply clarified by arranging *Testudo graeca* into a classification table as follows:

Kingdom:	Animalia	All animals
Phylum:	Chordata	Animals with notochord
Subphylum:	Vertebrata	Backboned animals
Class:	Reptilia	All reptiles
Order:	Chelonia	All turtles and tortoises
Suborder:	Cryptodira	Straight-necked turtles
Family:	Testudinidae	Typical tortoises
Genus:	*Testudo*	Eurasian tortoises
Species:	*T. graeca*	Mediterranean Tortoise

The word "picta" means "painted" and thus is the species name attributed to the Painted Turtles. Photo of *Chrysemys picta* by R. T. Zappalorti.

In the table you can see that turtles and tortoises form an order in the class of reptiles (as opposed to fishes, amphibians, birds, and mammals each of which forms a vertebrate class in itself). The reptilian class, in fact, contains four orders:

1. Chelonia: All turtles, tortoises and terrapins.
2. Crocodylia: All crocodiles, alligators and gavials.
3. Rhynchocephalia: The primitive, lizard-like Tuatara.
4. Squamata: Lizards, amphisbaenians and snakes.

As the orders are normally placed in evolutionary sequence, it follows that the turtles are

Sometimes a turtle will be the only species in its genus, a condition known as monotypy. Blanding's Turtle, *Emydoidea blandingii*, shown here, is a good example of such a turtle. Photo by K. T. Nemuras.

the oldest kinds of living reptiles. The modern order Chelonia contains two suborders, 12 families, about 75 genera, and some 220 species.

With the steady increase of our zoological knowledge, the science of taxonomy (the science of classifying living things) has been gradually improved. Nowadays there are strict regulations regarding the naming and publishing of newly discovered animal species and these are governed by the "International Code of Zoological Nomenclature", often referred to in short as "The Code". An international committee convenes at regular intervals to make decisions on whether a new species has been correctly named and to consider proposals for the changing of existing names brought about by reclassification in the light of new knowledge.

The provision of a clean-cut binomial to a species is not without problems however, and in some cases it is necessary to add a third name, making a trinomial. This is used when geographical groups of certain species show certain differences, but are not sufficiently different to be be considered as separate species. Such groups of animals are known as subspecies and, while many reptiles are regarded as just species (with a binomial), some may have quite a large number of subspecies. When a species is relegated to subspecific rank, the first (nominate) species described has its specific name simply repeated, while further subspecies are assigned a different subspecific name. Let's illustrate the point by taking a look at a genus of North American turtles.

The Alabama Red-bellied Turtle, of southern Alabama, USA, is

Very often an animal will be named after a specific individual, like Reeves's Turtle, *Chinemys reevesi*, named after J. R. Reeves, Jr., a British naturalist from the early 19th century. Photo by Dr. Herbert R. Axelrod.

considered to be a single species and thus has the simple binomial *Pseudemys alabamensis*. Conversely, the River Cooter, in the same genus, is considered to have two subspecies: *Pseudemys concinna concinna*, and *Pseudemys concinna texana*. Other species may have many more subspecies; in the same group, for example, Pond Slider, *Pseudemys scripta*, and the Painted Turtle, *Chrysemys picta*, both have four subspecies.

Specific and subspecific (binomial and trinomial) names are usually written in italic or underlined script to avoid confusion with common names or other parts the text in which they are cited. When it is necessary to use the binomials or trinomials several times in a given text, abbreviation is accepted provided it has been written once in full. Thus, *Testudo graeca* can be reduced to *T. graeca* and *Testudo graeca ibera* may be abbreviated to *T. g. ibera*.

When an animal is given subspecific rank, it is then given a "trinomial" name rather than a simple "binomial" name. Photo of *Pseudemys concinna suwanniensis* by R. D. Bartlett.

Some Turtle Biology

The name "terrapin" is basically nothing more than a synonym for "turtle," and usually only applied to the Diamondback Terrapins, genus *Malaclemys*, of North America.

Let us first of all clear up the difference between turtle, tortoise, and terrapin. We are all familiar with the turtle's general appearance: it has four limbs, a head at one end, and a tail at the other, but the most obvious feature (generally) is its box-like shell. North Americans tend to call all chelonians turtles although land turtles in the family Testudinae are more commonly called tortoises. Edible freshwater species have often been called terrapins (this term is thought to have been derived from an Amerindian word), but the name is now mainly restricted to one species, the diamondback terrapins, *Malaclemys terrapin*. In Britain the name turtle is generally used only for marine species, while terrapin is used for most freshwater species. Tortoise is used mainly for land species, but to further confuse the issue, some terrapins are referred to as pond or water tortoises. In Australia, where there are no land tortoises, they refer to their freshwater species as turtles or tortoises and use only turtle for marine species. In this book we will follow the American usage.

Turtles are normally regarded as the most primitive of the living reptiles, but in many ways the modifications required for life within a box-like shell make them, at the same time, highly specialized. The most outstanding modifications must be in the skeleton, which has had to adapt to containment within the shell. The shell itself has been reduced in some of the more recent genera. As most of the body vertebrae and the ribs are firmly attached to the shell, the pectoral and pelvic girdles lie inside the rib cage and the limbs emerge sideways through apertures in the sides of the shell. The acquisition of the shell was probably the reason for the limbs being fixed in a relatively primitive position.

The shell itself probably arose from an amalgamation of the rib cage and the scaly reptilian skin. There are two main layers: the dermal shell, which is the visible arrangement of horny plates, scutes, or laminae that takes the place of normal scales in other reptiles; and the bony plates, beneath which are a fusion of the ribs and vertebrae. Conventional reptilian scales may appear in chelonians only on the head and/or limbs or other areas of exposed skin.

The top part, or dome, of the shell is known as the carapace. The relatively flat area beneath is called the plastron. The carapace and

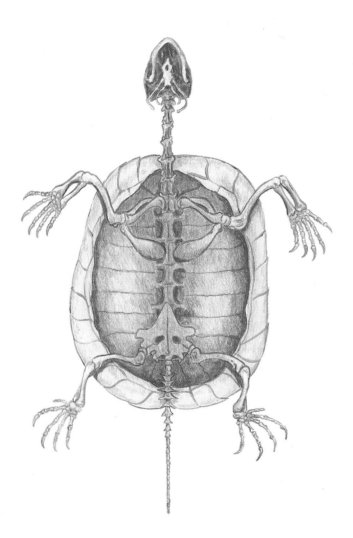

Underside of a typical chelonian skeleton.

plastron are joined at the edges, with apertures left for extension and retraction of the head and limbs. In some genera the plastron may be hinged near the allows the animal.to withdraw its head and limbs completely and shut itself away from the outside world. In one genus, *Kinixys*, the posterior part

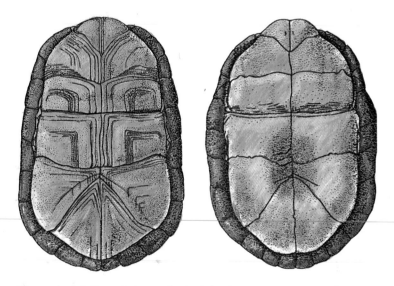

The main details and shape of a turtle's plastron can vary to some extent, but the basic pattern still remains the same.

front and rear (*Kinosternon* for example) or singly across the middle (as in *Emys*). The hinge is a transverse elastic joint across the plastron which of the carapace is hinged, giving added protection to the hind limbs when they are withdrawn.

The scutes on the shell are arranged in a

symmetrical pattern, but to enhance the general strength of the shell they do not correspond with the joints in the bony plates beneath. As the turtle grows, the epidermal cells between the upper and possible to estimate the approximate age of a turtle, but this cannot be considered exact since the rings tend to wear smooth with age and become indistinguishable. Also, in certain years, depending on

From this photograph you can clearly see some of the growth rings on this Eastern Box Turtle's, *Terrapene carolina carolina*, shell. Photo by L. Quinn.

lower layers form new rings of horny material around the margins of the individual scutes. By counting these rings it is weather conditions and temperatures, there may be two or even three growth periods, making more than one growth ring per annum.

The chelonian skull is relatively simple. The bottom jaws are fused at the chin. They have no teeth, but instead a tough, horny beak with very sharp edges which act in the manner of shears. There are no temporal fossae (lateral openings in the skull roof) as in other reptiles.

Turtles cannot breathe in the manner of other terrestrial vertebrates, as they are unable to expand and contract the chest. Some of the abdominal muscles are principally responsible for respiration that is also enhanced by pumping of the throat and movements of the head and limbs. The lungs are quite large and spongy and situated just below the carapace. It is thought that some freshwater turtles have accessory means of respiration by passing water over the mucus membranes in the throat and cloaca. Being richly

supplied with blood vessels, the mucus membranes act as gills, extracting oxygen from the water and allowing such turtles to remain submerged for relatively long periods.

The eyesight of most

Most turtles have relatively long necks and are able to stretch them quite far, but few can match the reach of the Snake-necked Turtle, *Chelodina longicollis*. The species name, unsurprisingly, means "long neck." Photo by Dr. Herbert R. Axelrod.

turtles is thought to be relatively good, while the sense of smell probably is also quite efficient. Sense of touch is well-developed, even on the shell. Hearing is probably relatively weak, though auditory perception may vary from species to species. In general, turtles are not greatly vocal, though the males sometimes emit screaming or grunting noises during copulation.

Chelonians have a

relatively long, flexible neck which (in most species) enables the head to be withdrawn into the shell for protection. The way in which the head is withdrawn separates the two chelonian suborders. In the suborder Pleurodira, the neck is bent sideways when the head is withdrawn, but in Cryptodira it is bent vertically. Pleurodirans are therefore popularly known as sidenecks. This suborder comprises the more primitive groups of chelonians which occur only in the southern continents of Africa, Australasia, and South America, though fossil forms have been found in North America and Eurasia. They are probably the most direct descendants of early chelonia which could not withdraw their heads at all.

The suborder Cryptodira includes most of the living chelonians and is divided by some workers into four superfamilies. These are:

1. Testudinoidea—Land tortoises; freshwater, box, snapping, and mud turtles
2. Chelonioidea—Marine Turtles
3. Carettochelyoidea— Pitted-shelled turtle
4. Trionychoidea:—Soft-shelled turtles

Turtles have colonized most suitable habitats and occur on all continents except Antarctica. They may be totally terrestrial, semi-aquatic, or mainly aquatic (all turtles must lay their eggs on land). Although all turtles show a basic shape, there is a great variety of color, form, and size. There are species that are mainly herbivorous, those that are omnivorous, and some that are mostly carnivorous.

Housing Your Turtles

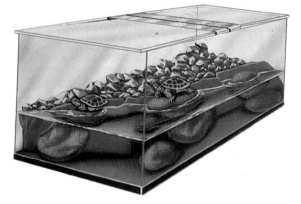

Virtually any hobbyist could set up an aquatic tank as simple and attractive as the one shown here. Artwork by Scott Boldt.

The kind of housing you provide for your turtles will depend on a number of factors, including amount of space available and finance, but accommodations can be conveniently divided into three broad categories depending on the type of chelonians you intend to keep. These are: housing for hardy land tortoises, housing for tropical land tortoises, and housing for aquatic turtles.

The three categories may be interchangeable to some extent in that hardy aquatic turtles may also be kept in the same enclosure as land tortoises, providing there is enough water available. Also, the amount of land provided for aquatic turtles will vary with the amount of time the species spends in the water. Those turtles, for example, which are almost totally aquatic (only venturing on land to rest or lay their eggs), can be kept in an aquarium tank, though if you want them to breed you will have to provide some dry land nesting sites, which we will discuss later.

HOUSING FOR HARDY LAND TORTOISES

When talking about hardy land tortoises we are thinking of those that live in temperate to sub-tropical areas and require a period of winter hibernation. Some of the European and American land tortoises, and some box turtles, fall into this category. At one time, when tortoises were easy to obtain, the reptiles were just given the free run of a suburban garden and allowed to forage for their own food. This would have

been fine if the garden was completely walled in, but more often than not, on some warm day, the tortoise would go marching

If you come to own a tortoise or box turtle of any kind, it would be in both your own and the animal's best interests to keep it outdoors during the warmer months. Photo by Susan C. Miller.

off and frequently never be seen again! Indeed, over the years I have heard of several people who have acquired a tortoise by it simply turning up in their back yard. After unsuccessfully trying to find the owner of the reptile they have then resigned themselves to adopting it. In many such cases of accidental acquisition the tortoise has probably fared much better than it would have done with its original owner.

Some wandering tortoises have often fared quite well on their own and may turn up in the garden of the original owner two or three years after they first disappeared. It is also very probable, however, that a high percentage of them would be unable to adapt to the alien climate, topography, and food supply, and eventually wither away in some quiet corner.

Nowadays, tortoises are much too valuable to allow freedom of the city. And by valuable we do not just mean monetary value, but also the value of the species themselves. Hardy tortoises can be kept very successfully in outdoor enclosures in climates much colder than their native ones, and with proper care and a few adjustments they will even breed prolifically. This has been admirably demonstrated by Professor Walter Kirsche, who for many years has been successfully breeding hundreds of southern European tortoises over several generations in the garden of his home at Paetz Ueber Koenigs Wusterhausen, just outside Berlin.

The simplest housing for a hardy tortoise or box turtle may consist of a circle of wire netting about 35 cm (14 in) high, pegged down onto the lawn, or even better, a weedy patch,

If you had a backyard large enough, you could conceivably start your own box turtle or tortoise colony! Note also the apple tree in the upper right corner. Once the apples fall to the ground, the animals could even feed themselves! Photo by Susan C. Miller.

which will give the inmates a choice of forage. Of course, the enclosure can be moved from one spot to another as forage becomes consumed. If the wire netting is attached to a sturdy wooden frame, the whole enclosure can be moved without the inconvenience of pulling out and relocating pegs. Remember that tortoises can burrow, so you may have to have the wire netting bent inward under the base framework, or even covering the whole floor; the tortoises will still be able to graze through the gaps.

If you have plenty of space, it is much better to build a more permanent enclosure. Since tortoises are not very adept at climbing vertical surfaces it is quite easy to construct a low (35 cm—14 in) wall with timber sleepers or paving slabs that are buried upright by about half their depth into the ground. To be even more permanent, a concrete foundation and a brick or block wall may be constructed. Some enthusiasts like to complement their turtles with hardy snakes or lizards. In such cases, the brick or block wall must be higher and should have an overhang at the top to prevent escapes. A continuous band of glossy material such as ceramic tiles or formica attached to the inside of the wall near the top will also help prevent any reptiles from getting a grip with their sharp little claws.

The size of the enclosure is immaterial but should be large enough for the growing edible weeds and plants to be able to replenish themselves after being eaten. For example, an enclosure 7 meters long by 5 meters (approximately 22 x 16 feet) would comfortably house four pairs of hardy tortoises or box terrapins. The interior

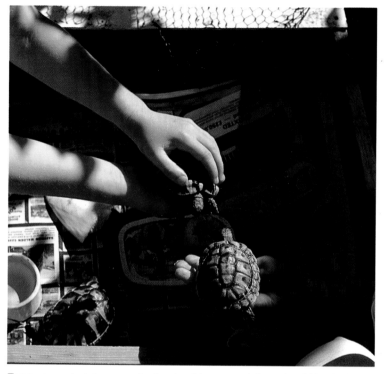

Even young tortoises can be kept outdoors, and they should be fed there as well. It is best however, to feed them separately from the adults. Photo by Susan C. Miller.

of the enclosure may be tastefully landscaped with rocks and slopes, but ensure that it receives adequate sunlight and also has areas of shade.

Cultivated plants, especially low shrubs, can be planted for shade, but also allow the weeds to grow. You can regularly plant the seeds of cabbage, lettuce, radish, and so on, and these will be greedily devoured by the tortoises as they grow. Ensure you have three or four sandy, sunny areas free of vegetation so the tortoises have a choice of nesting sites when they (hopefully) decide to breed.

The inmates should have a house, or even better a choice of two or three, in which they can rest and shelter from the rain, wind, or sun. These houses can also double up as hibernacula in the winter. They can be constructed from brick, stone, timber, or whatever, but should be insulated as much as possible. Prof. Kirsche provides his tortoises with timber and straw thatched huts, with deep layers of straw and peat moss on the floor inside. As winter approaches, the insides of the huts are further packed with hay and the whole hut is buried under a layer of leaf litter and straw.

Though the tortoises will find much of their own food, it will be necessary to offer them regular supplements. A covered feeding area is recommended so that food can be protected from the sun and rain. A shallow pool may be provided for tortoises and box turtles. This need not consist of anything more than a concrete slab driven into the ground, with a concave center about 5 cm (2 in) deep. Such a shallow pool is easily cleaned at regular intervals by scrubbing it with a stiff broom then just sweeping the dirty water out and replacing it with fresh water.

If you wish to keep aquatic turtles as well as land turtles, you must have a much deeper pool; but ensure that the margins of

Facing page: In the background you can see the wide variety of food items that tortoises thrive on. They are undoubtedly very eager feeders. Photo by Susan C. Miller.

Although designed primarily for fish, tanks like the model depicted here are perfectly acceptable for small aquatic turtle species.

the pool have a very shallow incline at all points, and no sheer edges, so that the tortoises can easily get out

should they happen to wander into the water. A filtration system and waterfall are ideal accessories, but in their absence the pond will need to be pumped out or drained and cleaned at intervals of about three months, depending on the amount of turtles there are. On hot days, some land tortoises like to bathe themselves in shallow water and may immerse themselves up to their necks.

HOUSING FOR TROPICAL TORTOISES

There are several options for housing tropical land tortoises and box turtles, and these will depend on the species, size, and number of occupants, as well as the amount of space, cash, and time available. During the warmer parts of the temperate summer, most tropical species may be kept in outdoor enclosures as

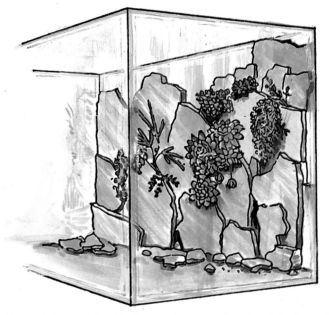

For certain small land turtles, a simple sand and rock tank may be acceptable. If they are captive-bred, they probably won't miss their natural surroundings at all.

described above. If you are lucky enough to live in a tropical or sub-tropical area you will, of course, be able to keep some of your tropical tortoises outside all year long. However, tropical tortoises in temperate climates usually have to be kept indoors for most of the time. Supplementary heating is also necessary and, in the case of desert dwelling species, this must be dry heat. Rainforest species and tropical box turtles, however, require a more humid atmosphere.

The simplest housing for some small tropical species

is a glass tank or terrarium heated with a normal tungsten light bulb, though this is best used only as a temporary accommodation if breeding is contemplated. By experimenting with light bulbs of various wattages (using a thermometer), you can arrive at a suitable temperature; most tropical tortoises require temperatures in the range 25-30°C (77-86°F). It is best to have the bulb at one end of the terrarium, and arrange for the highest temperature to be just below the bulb. This will mean there is a temperature gradient toward the other end of the tank that will allow the tortoises to find the spot where they are most comfortable. At night the heat can be turned off completely; the average indoor temperature in most dwellings is okay providing it does not drop below 15°C (59°F). In the wild habitat of some desert and montane species, the temperature

does drop rather dramatically at night, so this will be a natural phenomenon for them.

Other means of heating tanks and terrariums include heating pads, cables, and tapes. Some of the types of heaters used for aquariums and by horticulturists to propagate plants may all have their value. It is interesting to experiment with various types of heaters until you find your ideal system. If it is necessary to have the heating bulb on at night then it is best to have it concealed inside a tin can or an inverted clay flower pot. You can pass the electric wire through the hole in the flower pot or hole made in the base of the can and suspend the bulb inside the container by securing the wire with a clothespin. The bulb will then heat the container, which in turn will heat the air in the terrarium by radiation and convection.

As it is difficult to supply

indoor terraria with natural sunlight without overheating, it is best to supply a substitute. Perhaps the best type of substitute is a broad spectrum fluorescent tube, which will emit a good quality light containing a small amount of the ultraviolet rays which are beneficial to the health of your pets. Do not use straightforward ultraviolet lights, as these are too strong and can damage the eyes and skin of your turtles. You should aim for an equal photoperiod, that is 12 hours of light and twelve hours of dark for most of the year. You may make some seasonal variations of about 14 hours light and 10 hours dark for a few weeks in the summer, and then the opposite in the winter. This will help bring your turtles into breeding condition. The heating and lighting should work together. If you are electronically minded, or

know someone who is, it will be possible to rig up an automatic system of time switches, thermostats, dimmers, humidifiers, and so on, so that you can easily create and control any sort of climate your turtles require.

The interior decorations of a small terrarium are best kept relatively simple. Newspapers, or better still absorbent paper towels, can be used on the floor and then changed each time they become soiled. A very shallow water dish should be provided, preferably a heavy one so the inmates cannot tip it up. It is quite easy to make a shallow, heavy water dish with a sand and cement or concrete mixture; with a little imagination it can be made to resemble a natural rock pool.

THE TORTOISE TABLE

A very practical and attractive means of displaying your tropical

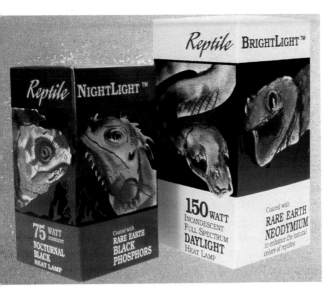

Providing your turtles with the correct photoperiod (day/night cycle) is very important. Photoperiod is often a factor in determining a herptile's behavior. Bulbs designed specifically for the keeping of reptiles and amphibians now are available at many pet shops. Some, like those shown above, provide not only light but a measure of heat as well. Both photos courtesy of Energy Savers.

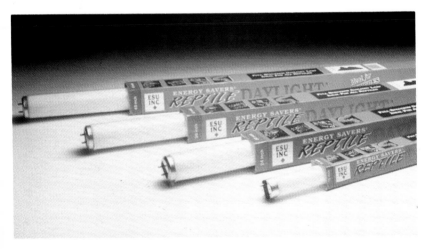

Organic substrates like crushed bark (left) are ideal for land-dwelling turtles. Such substrates are easy to work with, pleasing to the eye, and can be bought in bulk quantities. On the other hand, if you are looking for something simpler and not quite as naturalistic in appearance, a terrarium liner (below) will do the job. Both photos courtesy of Four Paws.

tortoises (or even temperate tortoises for most of the year) indoors, is on a tortoise table. An old timber dining table makes an ideal base on which to bring your pets nearer to eye level. To increase the area available to your tortoises you can use a large sheet of thick plywood, particle board, or similar, placed on the table. As plywood often is available in   sheets measuring about 2.4 x 1.2 meters (8 x 4 ft), this makes an ideal and spacious area for your tortoises. The board must have rising vertical sides made with planks or more plywood placed around its edges to prevent the tortoises from falling out. These perimeter planks must be just high enough so they cannot reach and scramble over; usually 25-40 cm (10-16 in). In order to facilitate viewing, one of the sides can be made of plexiglass (clear acrylic sheeting) or similar, although

sometimes such products can be rather expensive.

The tortoise table is best positioned near a south facing window (in the northern hemisphere; the opposite will apply in the southern hemisphere), or beneath a roof light, so that the tortoises can benefit from some sunlight. While the general ambient temperature of the average household is adequate for background warmth, a supplementary basking heat source will be necessary. The most ideal apparatus is a simple, infra-red heat lamp with a reflector shade. Such a lamp may be suspended about 60 cm (2 ft) above the table, and the beams of heat and light may be directed onto a spot on the substrate. The center of this spot will become quite hot, but there will be decreasing temperatures in concentric rings around the lamp so that the tortoises will be able to regulate their

Although the animals shown here are obviously not turtles, the point of interest is in the heat lamp. "Spot heating" is an excellent way to keep your pets warm.

temperatures by moving in and out of the heat, or remaining in a spot where the temperature is most comfortable to them.

While paper or similar can be used on the substrate, gravel is a much more attractive proposition. Large grade aquarium gravel or similar should be thoroughly washed by placing it in a bucket and swirling a jet of water through it until the effluent runs clear (you will require to do this several times with remove, replace, disinfect, and wash it about once per month. Gravel can be disinfected by first washing with water then placing it in buckets or other containers and immersing it in a 5%

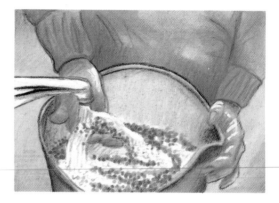

Before using any type of gravel, you should wash it thoroughly at least twice. Artwork by John R. Quinn.

several buckets of gravel). Then allow it to dry before placing it on the tortoise board in a layer about 2.5 cm (1 in) thick. Make sure there are no holes or gaps where the gravel can fall out and make a mess. It is advisable to have two lots of gravel so that you can solution of household bleach for 24 hours before swilling out and drying. As long as the droppings are scooped out on a daily basis, this monthly complete gravel change should be adequate.

Such a tortoise table should be made into an

attractive display feature in the room and may incorporate an indoor garden, a collection of cacti and succulents, or just a few pots of interesting plants. All pots must be fixed securely so that the tortoises cannot knock

A shallow, preferably heavy, water dish should be provided for both drinking and bathing. Needless to say, the water should be replenished at least once a day. Other decorations can include a couple of interesting rocks, logs, or

Since cleaning a turtle's tank can be a daily undertaking, decorating it simply is strongly advised. Artwork by John R. Quinn.

them over and reach the plants. Also, the pots should be high enough to prevent the tortoises from reaching the flora. One way of doing this is to partition off a corner with clay bricks placed high enough to prevent tortoises from reaching the top. Pots of plants can then be safely arranged behind the bricks.

branches; bleached driftwood or similar is particularly attractive. Not only do these decorations add to the decor, but they give the tortoises something to run around, clamber upon, or hide under, should they wish. Do not put any of these furnishings near the sides, as they may help allow your pets to climb the perimeter boards and fall out.

The tortoise table is most suitable for desert or warm temperate species, as the humidity in most centrally heated homes is often very low. At night the heat lamp or lamps can be simply switched off, as long as room temperature does not drop below 15°C (59°F).

A similar, permanent setup can be made at floor level in a conservatory or greenhouse, and one advantage of this is that you can have a drainable concrete pond set into the floor. The enclosure wall can be made from bricks, concrete blocks, or, if you want a less permanent feature, you can simply make an enclosure from four planks of wood.

A really substantial tortoise enclosure can be made from bricks and concrete in some alcove in the house. Such an enclosure, fitted with glass-framed viewing panels and doors, can have the interior kept at a high humidity for the benefit of tropical rainforest types such as *Kinixys* and *Cuora*. Means of maintaining a high humidity include adequate planting and regular mist spraying. A more reliable method is to have a thermostatically controlled aquarium heater and an aerator in the water container. A simple aquarium diaphragm pump will aerate and agitate the water and enhance the evaporation initiated by the water heating, thus increasing humidity in the air space.

HOUSING FOR AQUATIC TURTLES

Perhaps the simplest form of housing for aquatic freshwater turtles is a plain glass or plastic aquarium tank containing a few inches of water and a basking rock heated by a light bulb. Some pet shops sell specially made plastic turtle ponds suitable for very young turtles. Such accommodations would still require basking sites and have to be changed for larger housing as soon as the baby turtles outgrew them. Remember that the various species of turtles have varying amounts of aquatic behavior, ranging from almost totally aquatic to almost totally terrestrial. The almost totally aquatic species hardly ever come onto land except at egg-laying time, while the almost totally terrestrial types may limit their aquatic excursions to just paddling in shallow water.

The accommodations must thus reflect the wild habit and habitat of the species. Most turtles will generally thrive in some of the accommodations described for tortoises, but

Warming the water body of an aquatic turtle's tank is made easy when a keeper uses a fully submersible heater. Such heaters come in a variety of wattages and can be found in many pet shops. Photo courtesy of Hagen.

with additional amounts of water depending on the species. Some species can be upset and stressed by too much disturbance, so instead of frequent water changes, a filtration system may be installed. As most turtles are messy feeders and also produce copious amounts of droppings, the filtration system will usually have to be quite substantial. A mechanical filter of the type used for very large fish tanks is ideal. These usually consist of a container full of a filter medium (sand, charcoal, nylon wool, etc.) through which the water is forced and recirculated by means of a pump. Undergravel filters of the type used for marine and freshwater fish tanks are generally unsuitable for turtles due to the reptiles' continual digging of the substrate, an action that interferes with the filtration effect.

The filter must be cleaned every few days to remove sediment. You can tell when this requires doing because the flow of the recirculated water will slow down. The water will still have to be changed at intervals of say, three months, but this is considerably less than every few days, even daily, which would be the case if you had no filter at all. Keep in mind, though, that this is still the most efficient way of ensuring cleanliness, regardless of the rigors involved. Another relatively simple means of helping to keep the water fresh and prolonging the periods between complete water replenishments is to remove a jug or two of water each day and replace it with fresh water. Tap

Facing page: Effective filtration is of course a plus when keeping an aquatic turtle tank clean, but the water should still be changed at least once a week. Artwork by Lisa Marie O'Connell.

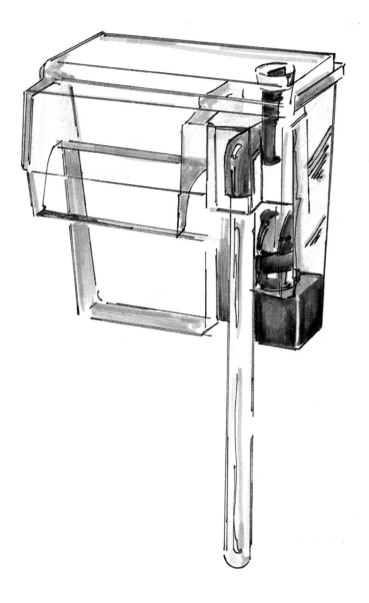

water is usually okay, but some types contain excessive chlorine which could irritate the skin of some species. To be on the safe side, it is then perhaps best to use rainwater, if available. Alternatively, tap water can be allowed to stand in a bucket for a few hours to allow the chlorine to dissipate by reacting with environmental elements.

THE OUTDOOR TURTLE POOL

Many species from temperate climates may be

Some turtles would probably appreciate the addition of a waterfall in an outdoor pool, provided of course you were willing to go to the trouble of putting one in. Artwork by John R. Quinn.

With just a few large stones, a little cement, and some basic masonry skills, anyone could produce an outdoor pool of this quality. Photo by Dr. Herbert R. Axelrod.

kept outdoors all year long in a suitable enclosed pool. This is an attractive and almost natural means of keeping turtles. They will behave in a natural manner and are more likely to breed in such a situation rather than in an indoor tank. Even tropical species may be kept in outdoor pools during the warmer parts of the summer, though you must ensure that they are safely indoors if there is any possibility of frost. An outdoor enclosure for turtles can be an aquatic modification of that described for land tortoises, but with a correspondingly greater amount of water.

The turtle pond should be at least 61 cm (24 in) deep at its deepest part. The pool and its corresponding areas of land must be totally enclosed to prevent escapes. The enclosure may be as simple or as substantial as you wish, ranging from pegged down or buried wire netting to planks or a solid brick or concrete block wall. Paving slabs buried about one third of their width into the ground and placed together to form a wall are also suitable. There are several types of ponds you could use, and a very simple temporary one can be made from a child's inflatable swimming pool with a pile of bricks in the center.

If you have the time and can afford the expense, an outdoor pond would make an extremely attractive addition to your yard's landscape. Photo by P. Hodgkinson.

Foods and Feeding

After only a few weeks in captivity, many turtle species will gladly take food right from your hand. Photo of *Pseudemys scripta elegans* by Susan C. Miller.

We all know that to stay healthy it is essential to have a balanced diet, one that has the variety and quantity of the constituents necessary to maintain both physical and mental health. These constituents consist of varying quantities of proteins, carbohydrates, fats, vitamins, minerals, and water. Like us, all animals including turtles require a balanced diet, and we can ensure that our pets get this by offering them a variety of foodstuffs. At one time it was thought that a herbivorous tortoise, for example, could make do on a diet of lettuce, with a little tomato. This was far from adequate however, and many tortoises lost so much weight that they were unable to survive through the winter.

In the wild, turtles forage for the variety of food they require. And although we are unlikely to be able to supply an exact replica of the natural diet, we can supply our captive specimens with perfectly adequate compromises.

FEEDING HERBIVOROUS LAND TORTOISES

Once accustomed to captivity, most land tortoises will accept a wide variety of food items. Although no turtles are strictly herbivorous, the staple diet of most land tortoises is green foliage. If allowed to run in a grassy, weedy pen, tortoises will find much of this greenstuff themselves. Many tortoises seem to be particularly attracted to yellow flowers, and a difficult, fasting newcomer can often be tempted to take its first meal by offering it dandelion flowers. Other favorite appetizers include strawberries, raspberries, bananas, and other soft fruits. When fresh fruit is unavailable, your tortoise will not turn its nose up at the canned variety.

Although your tortoise may be avidly consuming grass and weeds in the enclosure, it is advisable to give an additional

Facing page: Although most greens will be greedily accepted by many chelonian species, many of them need to be supplemented with something else. Photo by Susan C. Miller.

supplementary supply of varied items. A combination of two or more of the items listed further on should be given on a daily basis. Tortoises in indoor terraria with no access to growing greens should, of course, be given greater quantities of foodstuffs. For most of the smaller tortoises, I usually work on the principle of about one saucerful of mixed foodstuffs per tortoise per day. To make extra sure that your turtles are getting all of the necessary vitamins and trace elements, it is advisable to sprinkle a little powdered vitamin/mineral supplement over the food supply every other day. A weekly drop or two of cod-liver oil on the food will also do some good.

It is sometimes erroneously believed that land tortoises make excellent pest exterminators in your garden; this is a misconception. Tortoises will rarely eat live invertebrates except by accident; they are more likely to create havoc in your vegetable garden if they can get at it! However, tortoises will eat any odd bit of carrion which comes their way, and many captive land tortoises have developed a liking for minced, lean meat or canned dog or cat food. All the food you offer your tortoises should be first chopped into bite-sized pieces so that the tortoises do not have difficulty in eating it. Remember that in the wild, tortoises have the counter-leverage of plants anchored in the soil as they tear pieces off; something which is not the case in a saucer!

A mixture of several of the following food items, changed as the various items come into season, will provide your tortoises with a reasonably balanced staple diet, especially if supplemented with a good multi-vitamin/mineral

Danger! A human hand should never be allowed so close to a large tortoise. Many tortoises can give severe bites, even if they do not intend to. Photo by Susan C. Miller.

preparation: shredded lettuce, shredded cabbage, broccoli, grated carrot, sliced apple, sliced pear, sliced banana (including peels), sliced tomato, small cubes of wholemeal bread, cereals (with milk or without), clover, grass, dandelions, lean hamburger mince, and canned dog or cat food.

Tortoises suffering from stress, in quarantine,

requiring a tonic, or just plain difficult can often be persuaded to eat by offering one or more of the following treats (although it is not recommended that your pets be given these items all of the time, as they will likely become spoiled and then refuse the more conventional items of their diet): strawberries, raspberries, gooseberries, sweet grapes, peaches, apricots, nectarines, avocadoes, pineapple (not all tortoises will take to this but it is sometimes worth the try; even canned pineapple will do), young green peas or snow peas, runner beans, rose petals, dandelion flowers, milk thistle flowers and foliage, and clover. A little rose hip syrup, honey, or fruit jam diluted in water and sprinkled over the food, may also tempt them to feed.

It is very important that tortoises are able to develop adequate fat reserves before going into hibernation, and each reptile should gradually increase in weight through spring, summer, and early fall. If you think your tortoise has not put on enough weight for hibernation, then keep it in a heated, indoor accommodation and give it additional food until it is ready.

FEEDING AQUATIC AND SEMI-AQUATIC TURTLES

Most of the freshwater aquatic and semi-aquatic turtles are more carnivorous than herbivorous. Some, like the snappers and the softshells, are totally carnivorous, while some box turtles are omnivorous.

While many of the carnivorous turtles will eagerly take strips of lean, raw meat, this on its own does not constitute a balanced diet and must be viewed only as part of a more varied diet. Small turtles will take all types of

Freshwater shrimp are not often seen for sale as aquatic turtle food, but they make a fine dietary element nevertheless. Photo by H. J. Richter.

invertebrates and are especially fond of aquatic crustaceans such as small crayfish, freshwater shrimp, and the like. They will also take a wide variety of terrestrial invertebrates such as grasshoppers, spiders, slugs, and snails, all of which can often be found in the garden, especially if you search under stones and logs, etc. Earthworms are a favorite food for many species, and it is quite easy to set up an earthworm collecting station in most areas. Dig over a couple of square yards of soil, turning grass and weeds beneath. Place a 2.5 cm (1 in) layer of dead

In the wild, crayfish and shrimp are a very common part of many turtle species' diets. Photo of the shrimp *Macrobrachium rosenbergii* by A. Kochetov.

Pillbugs are one of the many turtle food items a keeper may be able to secure right in his or her own backyard. Photo of *Porcellio scaber* by Ken Lucas, Steinhart Aquarium.

leaves on top of this and wet them thoroughly with spray from a hosepipe or watering can. Then, cover the whole lot with dampened burlap sacks and leave it for about ten days. After this you should be able to collect earthworms from under the sacking at regular intervals provided you keep the area damp. After a couple of months of collecting you will have to give that area a rest and start a new collecting station elsewhere. By rotating various areas you should be able to get a continuous supply.

Some invertebrate foods are available commercially. Mealworms are an old standby item which have been cultured for many years. They are the larvae of one of the flour beetles, *Tenebrio molitor*, which are

In its adult form (shown here), the Giant Mealworm Beetle is a complete meal; in its larval form, however, it is not. Photo by Michael Gilroy.

really a pest to stored cereals but can be bred and used as a nutritious (although not complete) item on the diet of captive, insect-eating animals. Mealworms can be purchased in quantities by weight, and, if you do not require too many of them, it is perhaps best to purchase a few now and again. However, if you keep lots of small or juvenile turtles it will be well worth starting up your own culture. Keep your mealworms in a layer of bran in a shallow container with a close-fitting but ventilated lid (a large plastic lunch box or refrigerator container with a hole cut in the lid and covered with a piece of insect screening gauze or similar is ideal). Allow some of the mealworms to pupate and hatch into adult beetles, then place these in another container with about 5 cm (2 in) layer of bran or, even better, a mixture of bran and oats or another cereal. A piece of apple, carrot, or similar placed on the surface of the mixture and changed every two or three days will provide adequate moisture for the beetles. Best results will be obtained if you are able to maintain an ambient temperature of about 26°C (79°F) and a relative humidity of about 30%. The beetles will lay eggs which will hatch in about a week. It will be four to five months before the larvae reach sufficient size to feed to your turtles, so it is best to have two or three cultures going at any one time. The larvae, the pupae, and the adult beetles can all be used as food for turtles.

Crickets are another nutritious item which have become popular as culture insects. The species *Acheta domestica* and *Gryllus bimaculatus* are the best known. They are preferably

Crickets are perhaps the most common and very likely the most nutritious food item on the pet market available to turtles today. Photo by Michael Gilroy.

kept in a large plastic container (a plastic aquarium tank or even a plastic garbage bin with a lid will do). The container is partially filled with piles of newspaper rolls or empty egg cartons to provide adequate hiding places. The container should receive a (cabbage, lettuce, apple, carrot, etc.). The food should be replenished frequently to prevent spoiling. To breed the crickets, provide them with containers (empty margarine containers are ideal) filled with a moistened mixture of sand

There now are quite a few good commercially produced food items available to the aquatic turtle enthusiast, and such foods are available in a variety of sizes as well. Photo courtesy of Wardley.

normal day/night cycle for best results, and the temperature should be maintained at about 28°C (82°F). The crickets may be fed with saucers of bran, crushed oats, or other cereal, supplemented with finely chopped vegetables or fruits for moisture and peat or fine vermiculite, to a depth of about 7.5 cm (3 in). The adults will lay their eggs in this medium, which can then be removed to a separate hatching/ rearing cage. The eggs hatch into tiny nymphs in about one week and then reach adult size in seven to eight weeks. Adult-sized crickets are best for most turtles, though some of the smaller turtle hatchlings will be happier eating

rearing container, often are more carnivorous, and mature at a slower rate.

For larger carnivorous turtles, whole prey animals

Many turtles will accept freeze-dried food items after they have become comfortable enough with their captive surroundings. Such items can be bought in pet shops and many have the added advantage of being vitamin-enriched. Photo courtesy of Fluker Farms.

second or third instar nymphs.

Locusts (usually *Locusta migratoria*) are also available from biological suppliers and are very nutritious for your turtles, who will snatch them greedily from the water surface. These can be raised in a similar manner to crickets, though they will require a larger

are more preferable to raw meat. The whole prey animal contains fur and/or feathers and bone, both of which make an important contribution to the diet. Dead mice or day old chicks are also regarded as a delicacy, and if you have several turtles in the same enclosure then the prey animals can be given whole.

Hygiene and General Care

Hygiene goes hand in hand with the general care of your turtles. Poor hygiene and mediocre husbandry will soon lead to sickness, and even death, of your pets. Hygiene is the science of prevention of disease, and of course, the maintenance of good health. Many people relate the word hygiene to sanitation, disinfectants, and chemicals, but this is only part of the story. The most important aspect of hygiene is to provide captive animals with all they require to prevent stress. Most turtles are not greatly adaptable to alien surroundings, so sudden or prolonged changes in temperature, humidity, diet, or even terrain can cause stress that reduces resistance to disease. Many disease organisms may be present in the animals themselves, in the air, in the drinking water, or in the food. Healthy turtles kept in a stress-free environment will have immune systems in operation that prevent disease organisms from invading the body. Stress, however, can cause the animals' immune systems to fail, resulting in an outbreak of a disease that, in healthy, unstressed specimens, would have been automatically combated.

SELECTION OF SPECIMENS

Once you have decided on the species you would like to keep, the next step is to select an individual specimen or group of specimens. Surprisingly,

Eyes are a good place to look for early signs of disease. If they are as clear and clean as this Redbelly's, *Pseudemys rubriventris*, then you probably don't have much to worry about. Photo by K. T. Nemuras.

perhaps, this is also an important aspect of hygiene, as you should always ensure that your prospective purchases are healthy in the first place. When purchasing from a pet shop, for example, first impressions of the premises can give you a good idea as to the likely state of the animals in stock. Premises which are smelly, dirty, and untidy, and with overstocked cages, are more likely to nurture disease organisms than establishments whose proprietors obviously spend time to provide all the necessary requirements and display the animals in a way designed to impress the customer. A pet shop keeper should have pride in his chosen trade and not be just out to make a quick buck. If you are not impressed with the standard of hygiene in a dealer's premises or the attitude of the dealer in question, simply go to where you are more likely to obtain healthy stock and friendlier service.

As with any financial transaction, you must ensure you are getting value for your money. It is better to pay a little more for a healthy specimen than to save a few dollars on a suspect one. Make sure you examine each specimen very carefully before making a decision to purchase; check the carapace and plastron for damages or abnormal growth. Look for signs of ticks and mites on the skin, especially near the base of the limbs and in the folds around the neck. Ensure that the skin of the head, neck, and limbs is clean and unbroken. Ensure that the reptile is alert, clear-eyed, and plump; do not select specimens which feel excessively light in weight. Find out from the dealer if the animal is feeding regularly and what it is feeding on. Examine the nose, mouth, and vent for

This unpleasant-looking condition is actually rather common with turtles. It is an overgrown upper mandible, often the result of the animal not eating enough hard foods. Photo by William B. Allen, Jr.

signs of inflammation or discharges which could indicate disease. Most dealers will allow prospective buyers to handle stock for the purpose of inspection.

Other than purchasing your turtles from pet shops or specialist dealers in reptiles, there is a couple of other ways of obtaining specimens. One very good source is from the fellow

Everything about this turtle suggests good health: clear eyes, a clean shell, and skin which is smooth and unblemished. Photo of a hatchling Florida Redbelly Turtle, *Pseudemys nelsoni*, by R. D. Bartlett.

hobbyist who has already succeeded in breeding his other specimens and has surplus juvenile stock for sale or trade. A great advantage of such home-bred specimens is that since they are already accustomed to captive conditions they will probably have been handled from an early age and will thus be accustomed to people. The final method of acquisition is collection from the wild, and is one which should be considered with great caution. In most countries, many turtle species are protected by law and must not be interfered with in any way. In some countries, licensed collectors may be allowed to capture specimens. In some cases, only certain species may be protected while others may be collected by unlicensed persons. Before embarking on a collecting trip, be sure that you find out the appropriate legislation pertinent to the country, state, or area you intend to visit. Do not collect large numbers of turtles just for the sake of doing so or just because there are a lot in that particular area. Take only

There are a few turtles which cannot be kept by hobbyists due to their status on environmental protection lists. One of these is the Bog Turtle, *Clemmys muhlenbergii*. Photo by John M. Mertens.

what you can comfortably accommodate, and even then, be conservative. A single pair of turtles of a particular species should be adequate for most purposes.

TRANSPORTING YOUR TURTLES

In most cases, you will acquire your new specimens in your own neighborhood, and a fairly short car trip is all that is required to get them home to their new quarters. On such a trip, an open carboard carton with a little straw in the base will be adequate. However, longer trips require a little more forethought, especially when turtles are being sent by air or train. In the past, many turtles have perished during transit due to thoughtless packing. In recent years however, international cooperation on the humane transport of livestock has led to a more satisfactory situation. Ideally, tortoises and turtles

should be carried in single compartments in stout wooden boxes which have been packed with clean straw or hay for bedding. Choose the fastest and most direct transport route. During journeys of three days or less it is not necessary to feed or water healthy turtles (although aquatic species should have some moisture at all times), but try and send them when the weather is warm. Ensure that all boxes dispatched are adequately marked with the name, address, and telephone number of the consignee, plus any instructions to transporting staff (e.g., "Live Turtles—Please Keep Warm").

QUARANTINE

In order to prevent introduction of disease, all newly acquired turtles should undergo a period of quarantine before being introduced to your existing stock. The reptiles should be placed in a simple cage with the minimum of decorations in a separate room to the main collection. They should be fed and watered in the normal manner, and you should keep a close eye on them for at least 21 days. If no obvious symptoms of disease develop during this period, it should be safe to introduce the new turtles to those already in the collection. If the new ones are not feeding properly, or if they develop any suspicious symptoms while in quarantine, you should refer them to a veterinarian to ensure that any disease has been cured before you introduce them to your other stock.

HANDLING

There is often some dispute among turtle keepers as to how often their pets should be handled. In general, land tortoises are more suited to being handled than aquatic

Even a hardy turtle like this *Chelydra* shouldn't be picked up by its tail. Photo by Sally Anne Thompson.

turtles, which are best kept just for observation. Too much handling of some species can cause them stress and thus have an adverse effect on their health or breeding ability. Occasional handling of all captive turtles is, of course, necessary for inspection purposes. Some, such as the snappers and the softshells, can be quite belligerent, and large specimens are capable of giving serious bites—even to the extent of removing fingers—so beware! Large specimens should be picked up by both hands on the edges of the carapace, closer to the rear than the front, keeping your fingers well out of reach of the jaws. Some softshells are extremely lively and slippery, so a little practice will be required before you are adept at handling. Most small tortoises and non-aggressive turtles can be quite simply picked up with one or two hands. Always hold specimens near the floor or over a table (with a pillow or other soft padding on it) until you are sure you consistently have a good grip. Large, docile specimens should still be handled with a degree of thought though, since some can cause damage with their claws when struggling

to escape. I once had a very sore finger for a few days after an Aldabra Tortoise, *Geochelone gigantea* withdrew its limbs, catching my finger between the hind limb and the shell!

CLEANING

Cleanliness is essential in captive turtle accommodations if we are to combat disease. Terraria or aquaria should not only have all the necessary life support systems as described earlier, they also should be kept spotlessly clean. In dry land terraria, fecal pellets should be removed daily using a spoon or small shovel, and then the soiled spot cleaned thoroughly. About once every two weeks the turtles should be placed in temporary accommodations

Facing page: The Alligator Snapping Turtle, *Macroclemys temminckii*, is a particularly dangerous chelonian, having been known to take off a human finger or two. Photo by Peggy A. Vargas.

while the whole terrarium is thoroughly cleaned; gravel substrate materials should be removed and replaced. Dirtied materials can be disinfected and thoroughly rinsed with a hose. The interior of the terrarium should be scrubbed with warm soapy water and a mild disinfectant, such as a bleach or povidone-iodine solution, then thoroughly swilled out with clean water before being dried and refurnished. Water for drinking and/or bathing purposes should be changed very regularly (preferably daily) but more often if necessary. The glass viewing panels should also be kept crystal clear.

In aquaria for aquatic species, a complete water change will be necessary every two to three days unless you have an efficient filtration system. Even so, it will be necessary to change the water and the substrate gravel every two to three months, then clean the inside of the tank with a solution of bleach or povidone-iodine to remove slime and algae. It goes without saying that the filter should be cleaned out as often as necessary; and always remove uneaten food as soon as possible

HIBERNATION

Hibernation is a natural phenomenon. It is a period of inactivity caused by physiological changes that occur in some mammals and most lower vertebrates due to the onset of, and during, the cold winter months. It is an energy-conserving adaptation that enables the animal to survive at a reduced metabolic rate during times when food supply is inadequate. Turtle species from sub-tropical and temperate climates invariably hibernate in the wild for varying periods of time depending on the climate and the current weather situations. There is

Although the Wood Turtles, *Clemmys insculpta*, spend much of their time on land, they almost always hibernate deep in the mud of a nearby river bed, lake, or stream. Photo by Dr. Warren E. Burgess.

evidence to suggest that this period of hibernation is important for our turtles' health, especially with regard to their reproductive cycles. As temperature and photoperiod decrease in the fall, the animals will cease feeding and seek out a suitable spot in which to hibernate, this usually being in a burrow or similar, far enough below ground to be inaffected by frost or, in the case of some aquatic turtles, on the bed of a pond or river, sometimes even buried in the mud. The metabolism slows to such a rate that the oxygen requirement is very small. Water passing over the mucous membranes can supply adequate oxygen for those species that hibernate below water. Some species can withstand amazingly low temperatures provided they do not freeze.

In the past, many captive temperate turtles have been kept active in high temperatures throughout the year. The general opinion now is that non-tropical turtles should be given varying periods of artificial hibernation to enhance their lives and increase the prospects of breeding. Turtles in outdoor enclosures will, of course, seek out their hibernation quarters as soon as the weather dictates; it sometimes helps to increase the safety of these pets by stuffing their houses with straw and then piling more straw over the house or hibernaculum. The hibernating occupants will then emerge from their houses when optimum weather conditions return.

To hibernate a pet turtle in an indoor terrarium may seem a boring proposition, as it will not be seen for quite a long period. However, a short rest period at lower temperatures seems to be an adequate substitute for full hibernation (at least for some species). Only healthy, well-fed specimens should be hibernated. Toward the end of November (in the Northern Hemisphere) stop feeding your stock and gradually reduce the temperature in the terrarium over a period of several days. The minimum temperature will

Facing page: Young turtles are sometimes difficult to hibernate due to the fact that many are quite delicate and may not survive the rigors of winter dormancy. Photo of *Pseudemys rubriventris* by K. T. Nemuras.

Tortoises kept outside during the active season can be hibernated there as well, provided of course they are native to a temperate zone to begin with. Photo of *Kinixys belliana* by William B. Allen, Jr.

vary from 4°C (39°F) for temperate species to 10°C (50°F) for sub-tropical species. The photoperiod should also be reduced at the same time. The animals should be kept at these temperatures in an unheated but frost-free room for periods ranging from 4-12 weeks depending on their natural climatic zones. After the rest period, in mid-January to late February, the reverse procedure should be used to bring the temperature and photoperiod back to resemble spring and summer.

Most aquatic turtles wake from hibernation in reasonable condition, provided they were adequately fed during the previous season. However, some tortoises which are hibernated outside for a relatively long period may wake with their eyelids stuck together. This can be treated by holding the head firmly behind the occipital condyles (where the head joins the neck), so it cannot withdraw, and thoroughly swabbing the eyes with a boric eye wash solution on cotton wadding or lint. You may have to do this two or three times over a few days before the eyes are completely free and bright. If after about a week the condition persists, a professional should be consulted. Do not try to "force" the eyelids open if they are unwilling.

On emergence from hibernation, land turtles should be placed in a dish

Some tortoises are used to warmer climates, and thus should not be hibernated in the same fashion as those which are more northerly ranging. Photo of *Kinixys spekii* by K. H. Switak.

of lukewarm (20°C—68°F) water, as they are likely to be thirsty; and the warmth will help raise their temperature. They will usually not feed immediately, but you should remember that they must be thoroughly warm with a core temperature of 23-26°C (75-79°F) before they can feed efficiently. Those that consistantly refuse to feed should be more closely examined. Unfortunately, ulcers and infectious stomatitis are a common post-hibernative debilitation. On emerging, the turtle neither eats nor drinks because it has a sore mouth. The mouth must be opened in order to see the extent of the lesions on the tongue and so mucous membranes can be seen. Such an ailment is very serious, and if left untreated the turtle is likely to die. It will be necessary to consult a veterinarian, who will clean away the necrotic material, take a swab for bacteriological culture, and assist with rehydrating and supplementary feeding. Fluids, minerals, and vitamin replacements are the lifesaving nursing treatment that must be applied regularly over several months, as reptilian tissues are often slow to heal.

On emergence from hibernation, some turtles may be constipated. Cloacal irrigation with warm water can be most helpful, and the initial warm water bath at about 30°C (86°F) is often adequate to relieve this problem.

COMMON DISEASES AND TREATMENT

Turtles kept hygienically in a stress-free environment and receiving an adequate diet will remain remarkably resistant to disease. Many outbreaks of disease can be related to some inadequacy in captive management, so careful thought must be

Swollen eyes are a very common condition with captive turtles, especially those of the aquatic variety. This condition is usually caused by a severe lack of vitamin A. Photo by Dr. Fredric L. Frye from *Reptile Care*.

applied at all times to providing their needs. If it is suspected that all is not well with your turtles, a veterinarian should be consulted. Though many veterinarians are inexperienced in reptile medicine, most are able to make contact and extract advice from one who is. Some of the more usual problems are detailed below:

Nutritional Disorders: A common cause of sickness in many captive turtles can be put down to a deficiency (or sometimes an over-abundance) of certain dietary constituents. With a variety of the right types of food, vitamin and mineral supplements, and an opportunity to bask in sunlight (or an artificial substitute—ask about these at your local herp-oriented pet shop), the incidence of such conditions will be

The eyes of this very young Northern Diamondback Terrapin, *Malaclemys terrapin terrapin*, are just beginning to swell. This could be the first sign of a whole array of other problems. Photo by W. P. Mara.

minimized. A common condition with growing aquatic turtles is a swelling of the eyelids caused by a vitamin A deficiency. Injections of vitamin A (by a veterinarian) and supplementation of the diet with a good proprietory multi-vitamin supplement will produce a rapid response (although be

A break in the shell is naturally a very traumatic experience for both the turtle and the keeper, but surprisingly this condition can usually be treated with great success. Photo by Dr. Fredric L. Frye from *Reptile Care*.

careful not to overdo it—many herps can die from a disease caused by an overabundance of vitamins known as "hypervitaminosis"). Another common dietary deficiency in growing turtles is rickets, which can lead to a gross malformation of the shell. Caused by an absolute or phosphorus relative calcium deficiency, and often accompanied by a shortfall of vitamin D, it can be further complicated by a lack of ultraviolet rays from sunlight. This condition can be prevented quite easily by providing a varied diet of whole prey animals (both invertebrate and vertebrate), plus crushed cuttlefish bone or other calcium supplement, coupled with a good multi-vitamin/mineral preparation. Lack of natural sunlight or a good substitute (broad spectrum horticultural lamps or similar) is also a factor which affects the acquisition of vitamin D.

Wounds and Injuries: Though not strictly diseases, wounds may be caused by various factors and if left untreated are often susceptible to secondary infection. Turtles may have been tethered by one of their hind legs during capture, resulting in lacerations of the skin. Dogs and cats can chew or claw at the skin. Shallow wounds will usually heal automatically if swabbed daily with a mild antiseptic (such as povidone-iodine). Deeper or badly infected wounds should be treated by a veterinarian since in some cases surgery and suturing may be required. Fractured shells may occur if turtles are dropped onto a hard surface, are run over by vehicles, or have heavy objects dropped on them. A particularly unpleasant form of injury occurs when a turtle is accidentally run over by a lawn mower; this, unfortunately, is something

Fights with cagemates, rubbing against abrasive objects, and simple vitamin deficiencies can all cause ugly, weeping wounds. Fortunately, most of them are easily treatable. Photo by Dr. Fredric L. Frye from *Reptile Care.*

which is easy to do when a turtle is concealed in long grass. Some veterinarians are prepared to rebuild areas of shell with glass fiber, and perhaps repair broken limbs, though you may have a hard time trying to find such a vet. The practice of drilling a hole in a chelonian shell in order to tether the animal with string should be avoided. The shell is composed of living tissue and any injury will cause pain plus the possibility of secondary infection. Turtles which are loose in your backyard may occasionally hide under piles of refuse that you have planned to burn, so always check on the whereabouts of your pets beforehand.

Ectoparasites: These are

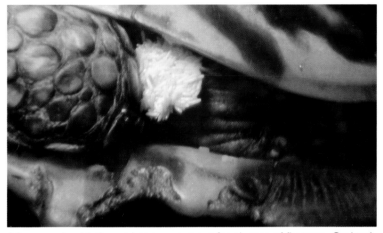

A keeper should always keep an eye out for clumps of fly eggs. On land-dwelling species, this occurs more often than one might think. Photo by Dr. Fredric L. Frye from *Reptile Care*.

parasites which attack external areas of the body in order to suck blood. Ticks and mites are the most common external parasites associated with turtles, especially land tortoises. Ticks are often found attached to newly captured specimens and may range up to 5 mm (1/5 in) in length. They fasten themselves with their piercing mouthparts to the turtle's skin, usually in a secluded spot under the edge of the shell, often around the vent, below the neck, or where the limbs join the body. Do not attempt to pull a tick directly out, as its head may be left embedded in the skin, causing infection later on. The tick's body should first be dabbed with a little alcohol (surgical spirit, meths, or even whiskey) to relax the mouthparts. The tick can then be gently pulled out with your thumb and forefinger, or more preferably, with forceps. Once all the ticks are removed from a wild-caught specimen, a further infestation in the terrarium is unlikely. However, there is a possibility of re-infestation with ticks if you keep your turtles in the backyard or other outdoor enclosure, so regular inspection of your pets' skin is important.

Mites are a more serious problem as they can often multiply to large numbers before they are even noticed. They usually prefer dry conditions and are therefore most commonly associated with terrestrial turtles. They do not necessarily stay on the reptile's body all of the time, but may hide in crevices in the terrarium. In great numbers, mites can cause stress, loss of appetite, anemia, and

Mites and ticks, the latter shown here, probably are the most common ectoparasites found on captive reptiles. Photo by Michael Gilroy.

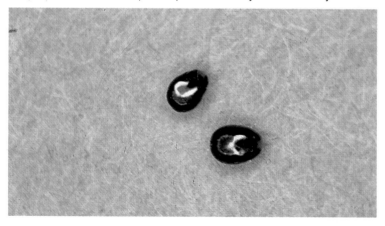

eventual death; they are also capable of transmitting pathogenic organisms from one turtle to another. The individual reptile mite is smaller than a pinhead, roughly globular in shape, and greyish in color, becoming red after it has sucked some blood. In a heavily infested terrarium, the mites may be seen running over the surfaces, particularly when you switch the lights on in the mornings and their tiny, silvery, powdery droppings may be seen on the turtles' carapaces. Mites are most often introduced into the terrarium through new stock (another good reason for quarantine and careful inspection).

Fortunately, mites can be quickly eradicated by using a proprietory plastic insecticidal strip (of the type used to control houseflies). A small piece of such a strip placed in a perforated container and suspended in a terrarium will kill off free-moving mites. Remove the strip after three days, then repeat the operation ten days later to kill off any newly hatched mites. Two or three treatments will usually destroy all mites in the terrarium and on the turtles. If mites should infest an open-topped tortoise table, you should remove the tortoises to an enclosed terrarium for insecticidal strip treatment. Then remove all materials from the tortoise table and dispose of them by burning, or sterilize them by boiling. The tortoise table and adjacent areas should then be sprayed with a contact insecticide, ensuring that all nooks and crannies in the construction are covered. Leave for one hour and scrub out with warm soapy water, then rinse and dry thoroughly before refurnishing and reintroducing treated tortoises. Your veterinarian may be able to advise a

Ectoparasites can be found virtually anywhere on a host's body. Photo of a tick on a Gopher Tortoise, *Gopherus polyphemus*, by R. T. Zappalorti.

miticide which can be applied directly to the turtles either by spraying or bathing but be sure to use only products recommended for direct application to animals.

Endoparasites: These are organisms which live inside the body, usually in the alimentary tract. Those that are most likely to infest our turtles are roundworms and tapeworms. In the wild, turtles are almost all infected with worms of one form or another, and in most cases there is no danger to the reptiles. However, during times of stress (capture for example), normal resistance to the worms will be reduced, triggering a massive increase in size or numbers of worms, causing anemia, general lethargy, loss of appetite, and eventual death. Routine microscopic examination of fecal samples by a veterinarian will reveal infestations. There are several proprietary brands of vermicides available through your veterinarian which may be offered with the food, or in severe cases via stomach tube.

Bacterial Infections: There are many forms of bacterial infections which can attack turtles, especially if they are kept in unhygienic conditions. Infective salmonellosis is an intestinal disease which has been known to have been transmitted from reptiles to man (especially from freshwater turtles), so it is important to thoroughly wash your hands after each cleaning or handling session. Salmonellosis manifests itself in the watery, green-colored, foul-odored feces. Consult a veterinarian, who will probably treat the infection with an antibiotic.

Protozoan Infections: Various enteric infections can be caused by protozoa, including *Entamoeba invadans*. If untreated, the

This condition is probably as painful to the turtle as it looks. It is an ulcerative disease that mainly attacks aquatic species. Photo by Dr. Fredric L. Frye from *Reptile Care*.

disease can rapidly reach epidemic proportions in captive reptiles. Symptoms include watery, slimy feces and general debilitation. Treatment with metronidazole (by a veterinarian) via stomach tube has proved effective for this and other protozoan infections.

Fungus Infections: Occur mainly in aquatic turtles, though they may occur under accidentally loosened carapace scutes in land tortoises. Such infections are fortunately quite rare, usually appearing on specimens that are already stressed by other factors. Regular shedding of the shell scutes is normal among many growing aquatic turtle species, but when partial shedding occurs due to stressful conditions, it provides sites

Note the bubble coming out of this Painted Turtle's, *Chrysemys picta*, mouth. Often this is an early sign of respiratory disease. Photo by Dr. Fredric L. Frye from *Reptile Care*.

open to mycotic (fungal) and other infections. Spongy material under scutes, and/or a white growth on and around the scutes, are symptoms of such infections. Caught in their early stages, fungal infections can usually be cured by administration of fungicidal treatment such as immersion in a very weak mercurochrome solution (0.0005%) for three days, then three days in fresh water, then repeat. Severe cases may require surgical removal of infected tissue and a course of anti-fungal drugs as advised by your veterinarian.

Repiratory Infections: Though relatively uncommon in turtles, respiratory infections may manifest themselves in stressed specimens, especially land tortoises and box turtles. The patient will have difficulty breathing, the nostrils will be blocked, and there will be a visible nasal discharge. Often the symptoms can be alleviated by moving the patient to warmer, drier, well-ventilated quarters. More serious cases will require antibiotic treatment from a veterinarian.

Weight/Length Ratios in Tortoises: British

veterinarian Dr. O. F. Jackson examined many European tortoises (*Testudo* species) and came to the conclusion that the weight/length ratio could be correlated with the clinical condition of the reptile. The ratio figure is arrived at by dividing the total body weight of the tortoise (in grams) by the length of the

Sometimes a turtle affected with a respiratory disorder will swim lopsidedly. Usually the affected lung will be on the lower side. Photo by Dr. Fredric L. Frye from *Reptile Care*.

carapace between the verticals (in millimeters).

For example, a specimen of *Testudo graeca* in excellent clinical condition weighed 2055 grams and had a carapace 235 mm in length, giving it a ratio of 8.7. In fact, the optimum ratio for *T. graeca* in excellent clinical condition would be 8.6±0.7 and a specimen would be expected to be within these parameters at the end of the summer season prior to hibernation. An average condition *T. graeca* would have a ratio of 6.4±2.0. (perhaps post-hibernation to early summer) while a specimen in sick, anorexic, or poor clinical condition would have a ratio of 3.3±0.9 (such a specimen would require urgent diagnosis and treatment and probably would not survive a period of hibernation). Other species studied had slightly different ratios. For example, *T. hermanni* in excellent clinical condition would have a ratio of 7.8±0.9. There is no reason to doubt that similar optimum weight/length ratios in most other chelonian species could be calculated, though ratios would vary quite dramatically depending on species, type and weight of shell, habits, and so on.

Reproduction
and
Captive Propagation

As techniques for captive breeding become more and more reliable, more species are offered as young rather than wild-caught adults. Photo of *Clemmys guttata* by W. P. Mara.

Every turtle keeper should make captive propagation of the specimens a major aim. It is now almost impossible to obtain many species from the wild, as they are rightly protected in their country of origin. In any case, further collection from the wild could be an additional threat to the continued existance of many species. We will therefore have to rely increasingly on captive-bred stock in order to satisfy the demands of the chelonian enthusiast. Unfortunately, turtles are still not as easy to breed in captivity as, say, rabbits or budgeriagars. One reason for this is because relatively little research has gone into turtle breeding compared with more popular pets. Another reason is that reptiles are much more environmentally and climatically oriented toward reproduction than many domesticated mammals and birds. Fortunately, however, some relatively recent research has shown that turtles may be not quite as difficult to breed as previously thought. Of course, breeding turtles does require quite a bit of effort, patience, and time from the keeper. In this chapter we will briefly discuss the general aspects of reproduction and captive breeding.

DETERMINATION OF THE SEXES

One very important aspect of turtle breeding is the fact that you must obviously have a male and a female before you have any hope of captive breeding. The sex determination of many species is quite difficult, but becomes easier with practice. General methods which are not always reliable include the fact that a male may have a concave plastron (to accomodate the female's carapace during copulation) while the female's may be flat. The male's tail is usually much longer and thicker than that of the female, while the vent sometimes appears to be in the tail itself rather than at its base (as in the female). In many aquatic turtles, females are considerably

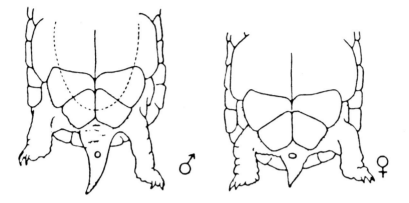

Differences in tail shape are one way to make a fairly good guess as to the sex of a turtle, but such techniques are not entirely dependable.

larger than the males, but this rule may be reversed in some box turtles or land tortoises.

In most species the sexes are similarly colored, but there are a few exceptions. In the case of the Spotted Turtle, *Clemmys guttata*, for example, the male has brown eyes and a tan chin, while the female has orange eyes and a yellow chin. In both the Eastern and Western Box Turtles, *Terrapene carolina* and *T. ornata*, the males have red eyes while those of the female are yellowish brown. The males of certain species have particular sexual dimorphisms, including elongated foreclaws, spine-tipped tails, or pointed snouts.

COURTSHIP AND MATING

The different habitats of the many species result in varied stimuli being required to bring turtles into a mating mood. With many temperate species it seems to be the increased

Very often a captive turtle will need no encouragement to breed whatsoever. Many are perfectly willing on their own. Photo of *Terrapene carolina* by Elaine Radford.

photoperiod (length of daylight) and the warmth of the spring sun after the winter period of hibernation or low activity that trigger the release of sex hormones into the bloodstream. Once in a mating mood, nothing seems to stop the males from searching out females and attempting to court them.

In land tortoises, some courtship appears to be rather violent. Not only does the male batter the female's shell with the front part of his carapace, he will also bite her quite severely in order to get her into submission. On encountering a female, he will start bobbing his head before approaching her. Then he plants his feet firmly on the ground, extends his limbs to their full capacity, and withdraws his head before swinging his shell energetically in the direction of the female and butting her shell sharply with the front part of his carapace and/or plastron. He may do this several times in quick succession, stopping occasionally to catch his breath before starting again with renewed vigor. In areas where the tortoises are common in the wild, this sharp tapping noise is a familiar springtime sound that emanates from the vegetation of the meadows and hillsides. Unfortunately for the tortoises, this was once an invitation for peasants, who collected them for food. Since the female tortoise at first never seems particularly enthusiastic about the male's attentions, he will recourse to biting her limbs; sometimes so violently as to draw blood. Initially the female may try to make her escape, but he pursues her energetically, butting and biting until she submits (by sitting still).

Since male turtles are not particularly choosy about their mates, it is always a good idea to have more than one female available. Photo of *Terrapene carolina* by Elaine Radford.

Due to the bulbous shape of some turtle   shells, the males usually have to make quite an effort to mate. Artwork by John R. Quinn.

This is the signal for the male to begin the process of copulation. He mounts the female from behind with his concave plastron curving around her carapace as he pushes his tail under hers. The male's tail is longer and thicker than that of the female and contains the penis which, during mating, is extruded from his vent and inserted into hers in a corresponding position below her tail. To achieve satisfactory intromission, the male often has to incline his body vertically

In some of the emydid turtles, courtship consists of males swimming in circles around the females and caressing them until they are put in a submissive mood. In some *Pseudemys* species, the males have elongated claws on the forelimbs that are used to gently caress the female's face. Some of the mud and snapping turtles have virtually no courtship behavior, and the male simply overpowers the female. In some species with low carapaces, the male may grip the edge of the female's plastron with his forelimbs during copulation. In species with high-domed shells, the hind limbs only are used to grip. Aquatic turtles usually mate in the water, often coming up for air several times during copulation. The duration of copulation may be as little as five minutes, to one hour or more. In some species, especially the land tortoises, the males are extremely vocal during copulation, letting out loud bellows, grunts, and hisses.

EGG-LAYING AND INCUBATION

Egg-laying takes place 6-10 weeks after mating, depending on the species. In a few species, the females are able to store sperm for some considerable time and do not need to mate every

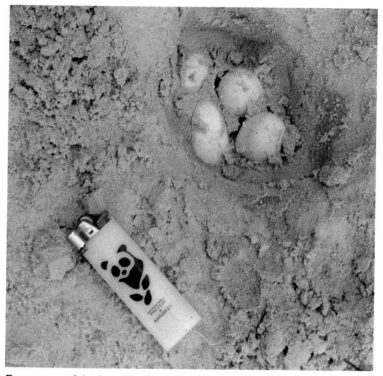

Even some of the larger turtle species have very small eggs. Photo of the eggs of a sideneck turtle, *Podocnemis*, by Dr. N. L. Chao.

season. All species have to lay their eggs on land and all of them bury their eggs in one way or another. Land tortoises generally excavate a hole in some suitable spot where the surface will be warmed by the sun. As in all turtles, the excavations are done with the specially flattened hind feet. Many river turtles excavate holes close to river banks, while others may leave the water

Unlike many other herptiles, most newborn turtles look almost exactly like their parents. Artwork by John R. Quinn.

to nest some considerable distance from it. In some cases, eggs may be placed under decaying vegetation or deposited in the burrows of other animals. The eggs are usually painstakingly covered with earth and vegetation before they are left. Fluid is often passed from the cloaca during excavation and/or over the material covering the eggs. This may help soften the earth, provide additional moisture, and in some cases help compact the plug that fills the nest cavity. Some species divide their egg batches between two or three nest sites, while others may make two or more false nests to confuse predators.

Number of eggs per breeding season varies from one or two (in the African Pancake Tortise, *Malacochersus tornieri*) to a thousand or more in some of the marine turtles (in several clutches, with intervals in between). Eggs are white in color and, depending on the species, the shells may be soft, leathery, and water absorbent, or hard, brittle, and relatively impermeable. They may be round or elongate and vary in diameter from 1.5 cm to 7.5 cm (1/2 in to 3 in) depending on the size of the species. Temperatures required for incubation range from about 26-33°C.

Research with some species has shown that the sexes of the hatchlings can be determined by the ambient incubation temperatures. For example, the eggs of the Loggerhead Turtle, *Caretta caretta*, will produce equal numbers of males and females if incubated at 30°C (86°F), but basically you should hatch out all males at 28°C (82°F) and all females at 32°C (90°). There is evidence to suggest that this phenomenon exists in many other species, but as the natural incubation temperatures generally fluctuate between the extremes, the sexes in population hatchings usually turn out in approximate equal numbers. Incubation time is also dependent on temperature and species. In general, a temperature at the higher optimum extreme will allow a shorter incubation time. Most incubation times are in the region of 50-70 days, especially in temperate species. With some tropical species however, this period may be as long as 150-400 days. In such cases, development can temporarily halt when conditions are unsuitable (in times of drought for example). In other cases, hatchlings are unable to leave their nests immediately, due to cold weather. Some North American river turtles, for example, may hatch in the fall and spend their first winter in hibernation right in the nest. Some tropical species hatch and may be unable to escape from the nest until rain softens the hardened soil covering the nest.

ARTIFICIAL INCUBATION

As captive turtles usually lay their eggs in climates or sites unsatisfactory for normal development, it is generally necessary to remove them to facilities for artificial incubation. The eggs of temperate, sub-tropical, and tropical species will not normally hatch naturally in outdoor enclosures in northern temperate areas (the reverse applies, of course, in the southern hemisphere), so after allowing the turtle to lay and cover her eggs and move away from the site, the eggs should be carefully excavated from the nest. Always keep a close eye on your pets when you suspect they are about to lay eggs so that you can be sure

More often than not, a yolk sac will still be attached to a neonatal turtle. This should under no circumstances be removed by the keeper. Artwork by John R. Quinn.

where the eggs are concealed. Many turtles are quite clever in hiding their clutches, and if you do not witness oviposition, especially in an outdoor enclosure, you are unlikely to discover the eggs or indeed even be aware of them. Most enthusiasts advocate keeping the eggs in the position in which they were laid and mark the "top" with a water-based marker.

The collected eggs are placed in an incubation medium, which may be damp sand, sphagnum moss, or vermiculite. The latter has proven to be a very efficient medium. It is a clean, inert, granular material much used in the insulation and horticultural industries. When using vermiculite, add an equal volume of water and press out any excess through a fine sieve. A 5 cm (2 in) layer of this moistened material placed in a plastic ice cream tub or similar will make an ideal incubation container. The eggs are buried to about a three-quarter depth into the medium, with the upper, marked part exposed. The tub is placed in an incubator or other area where the temperature can be maintained at about 30°C (86°F). Ensure that the vermiculite does not become too dry during

Even some of the "nastier" species, like these Snapping Turtles, *Chelydra serpentina*, can be reared into tolerable pets if acquired at birth. Photo by William B. Allen, Jr.

incubation. An occasional mist spray of the medium surface will help to maintain moisture levels. At the same time, care should be taken not to waterlog the medium, as this could result in suffocation of the embryos, which absorb oxygen through the walls of the egg shells.

Chelonian eggs should be kept in the same position during incubation, and it is generally accepted that they not be turned as one would turn birds' eggs. To keep out excess light from the incubation bulb (if used), the container of eggs can be covered with a piece of sacking or other open-weave cloth. Do not disturb the eggs, but inspect for moisture content of the medium daily.

A simple incubator can be made by using a glass-fronted wooden box. A few small ventilation holes should be drilled in the sides and the top. A 100 watt bulb (preferably colored blue or red to reduce light intensity) is placed in a socket attached to the inside of the ceiling or wall. A thermostat placed near the egg container is set at 30°C (86°F), this being an optimum temperature for most species—do not start trying out sex ratio experiments with varying temperatures until your incubation techniques are perfect!

Here is one method of hatching tortoise eggs without the use of an incubation medium that has proven very successful: the eggs are placed in holes drilled in an acrylic sheet mounted over a large flat dish of water, which is heated by a thermostatically controlled aquarium heater, and all contained within an outer container. Alternatively, a plastic or glass aquarium tank can be used with water in its base. The relative humidity in the container remains high and

The egg tooth is perhaps the most important part of a turtle's anatomy during hatching. It enables them to tear through the tough, leathery material their eggs are made of. In this photo of the Red-eared Slider, *Pseudemys scripta elegans*, by William B. Allen, Jr., the tooth is quite apparent.

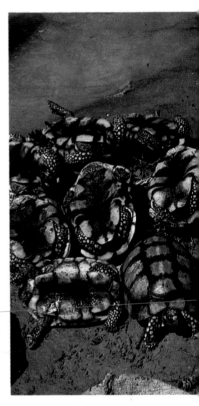

Photo of a group of young Yellow-footed Tortoises, *Geochelone denticulata*, by Harald Schultz.

the temperature can be finely adjusted. A sheet of glass placed at an angle above the eggs will ensure that any condensed water does not fall on the eggs.

When ready to hatch, a young chelonian makes a slit or hole in the egg shell with its egg tooth (a sharp projection on the tip of its snout). The egg tooth is lost shortly after hatching. Hatching may take from a few minutes to several hours, but eventually the shell will be broken wide enough for the hatchling to wriggle free. Ensure that there are no dangers for the hatchlings at this stage in case you are unable to keep an eye on them. In water-heated incubators, for example, ensure that there is nowhere for the hatchlings to fall in the water; even some aquatic species can drown in the early stages if they do not have a sloping landing site! On hatching, the yolk sac (the part of the egg that provides most nutrients) will still be attached to the center of the plastron. Do not attempt to remove this

the turtle should be placed in a shallow dish of lukewarm water and gently swabbed until the egg shell breaks free.

REARING

In the past, rearing of hatchlings has often posed greater difficulties than the hatching of the eggs. This was due to an ignorance of the nutritional requirements of young turtles. Diets that are poor in nutrients and those which are too rich can both cause problems. One very common problem in the rearing of small aquatic turtles was the swelling of the eyelids and eventual blindness due to a deficiency of vitamin A. Other problems included rickets and malformation of the shell due to various deficiencies. A good, balanced diet as described earlier in the text, but modified to take the small size of the juveniles into account, will ensure that

sac or interfere with the hatching process; allow nature to take its own course. On very rare occasions, a slow hatchling may become cemented to the egg due to the albumin drying out. In such a case these problems are diminished. With aquatic turtles, try and give a variety of invertebrate foods, including mosquito larvae, tubifex worms, small crustaceans, etc. Pieces of ox-heart or lean meat should be cut into very small, bite-sized portions. Juvenile land tortoises should also be given a varied vegetable diet chopped into very small portions; supplement this with some animal matter such as lean hamburger meat or tiny pieces of cooked chicken. Baby aquatic turtles may be reared in small, plastic aquarium tanks with shallow water and a large, flat, basking stone. Juvenile land tortoises can be kept in similar small accommodations, with a paper or coarse sand substrate. As some adult turtles are not to be trusted, never leave them together with hatchlings.

Note the immense size difference between these two tortoises. The top one is *Psammobates tentorius*, and the one beneath, *Geochelone pardalis*. Photo by K. H. Switak.

A Selection of Species

In the following text I intend to introduce the reader to each of the turtle families and to a selection of genera and species. Those, such as the marine turtles that are unlikely to be kept in the home will be only briefly described, but those that are frequently kept as pets in the terrarium or aquarium will include factors on their general care and breeding. English names and some alternatives are given when possible, but bear in mind that such names may vary from area to area. Lengths given indicate the length of the carapace and are the maximum that someone can expect in an adult specimen of the species being described.

SUBORDER CRYPTODIRA

FAMILY CARETTOCHELYDIDAE

This family contains only a single genus and a single species that, until quite recently, was not well known.

Carettochelys insculpta has been variously described as the Fly River Turtle (after its haunt in New Guinea), the Pig-nosed Softshell Turtle, the Pitted-shell Turtle, and the Plateless River Turtle and is a good example of how important scientific nomeclature can be. Known initially only from the river systems of Southern New Guinea, it was found relatively recently also in

Perhaps the most outstanding characteristic of *Carettochelys* is its piglike nose, obvious in this photograph by K. T. Nemuras.

the river systems of northwestern Australia. It may be found in lagoons isolated by the dry season. It has a maximum carapace length of 61 cm (24 in) and is colored uniformly gray-brown to dark olive above and off-white to yellowish below. There is a whitish streak between the eyes. The shell is covered with a soft, pitted skin, not unlike that of some of the true soft-shells. The limbs are paddle-shaped and reminiscent of those of marine turtles. The snout is fleshy and shaped like that of a pig.

Known to many as the Pig-nosed Turtle, *Carettochelys insculpta* is also often referred to as the Fly River Turtle. Photo by Peter Pritchard.

The turtle is very aquatic, females only emerging at the end of the dry season, usually at night, to lay about 15 round, soft-shelled eggs in a hole excavated in high sandbanks. Husbandry is poorly documented and, like marine turtles, it probably does not make a good captive. If it must be kept, a large, heated aquarium or indoor pool should be used. This species is omnivorous and will take carrion, fish, and some fruits. In the wild it is said to consume figs and the fruits of the pandanus palm.

FAMILY CHELONIIDAE

This family contains four genera and six species of sea or marine turtle. Although it is unlikely that sea turtles will ever become popular pets in the home (their requirements are such that it would be impossible to provide them with optimum conditions), they are extremely interesting animals in their own right. The turtle enthusiast will always have a soft spot for the marine turtles even if he or she cannot keep them.

Sea turtles differ from freshwater species in the way they move through the water. While the majority of river and pond dwellers paddle along with alternating motions of their webbed feet, their marine cousins seem to fly through their salty environment, with broad front flippers beating simultaneously like the wings of a bird. The rudder-like rear flippers are used for turning and braking. Sea turtles show quite an amazing turn of speed, some having been clocked in excess of 20 m.p.h.

All sea turtles are listed by CITES (Convention on International Trade in Endangered Species) as endangered and they are protected in most countries. However, turtles are still

Regardless of the fact that most sea turtles do not have much interaction with man, they still seem comfortable in his presence. Photo by R. Juriet.

The Hawksbill Turtle, *Eretmochelys imbricata*, is strictly a tropical sea turtle, having been recorded nesting on North American beaches perhaps no more than a dozen times. Photo by Dr. Herbert R. Axelrod.

exploited illegally in many areas—a difficult problem to overcome particularly when it applies to people who have always regarded the flesh of turtles and their eggs as legitimate items for the menu and their shells for ornamentation and profit.

Sea turtles are circumtropical in distribution, but extend sporadically into sub-tropical and temperate oceans. They range in total length from 80 cm (32 in) in the Atlantic Ridley Turtle, *Lepidochelys kempii*, to 200 cm (78 in) in the Loggerhead, *Caretta caretta*, although such large specimens would now be very few and far between.

The weight of such a large specimen would be in excess of 454 kg (1000 lbs)! The general body form of the family members includes a low, streamlined carapace covered in scutes. The limbs are flipper-like and the head cannot be withdrawn into the shell.

Most sea turtles are carnivorous, feeding on a wide variety of marine animals including molluscs, barnacles, crustaceans, jellyfish, sponges, sea urchins, and fish. The adult Green Turtle, *Chelonia mydas*, is an exception that grazes extensively on sea

After years of study and field research, it is now believed that the mortality rate among young sea turtles is alarmingly high. Photo by R. T. Zappalorti.

grass. Sea turtles migrate over great distances between feeding and nesting areas and the females reproduce in one to three-year cycles. Nesting areas are high up on sunny tropical beaches. Nests may be few and far between or in great numbers. A gravid female must leave the surf and drag herself laboriously up the beach, usually at night, to just above the high water mark. With her rear flippers she then excavates a deep hole in the sand before laying her eggs. Usually about the size of ping-pong balls, the eggs are globular, white, and parchment-shelled. Numbers of eggs may range from 80-200. Some species may lay several clutches over a period of 30-40 days with a total number of 1000 or more! After covering her eggs with the excavated sand, the female returns to the sea.

Sea turtles often have favorite nesting beaches described as "rookeries" sometimes with hundreds of nests. An important factor in the conservation of these reptiles is the protection of the nesting beaches from human predation, and in some countries, armed guards are employed to keep a 24 hour watch on beaches during the breeding season. Once the tiny turtles (rarely more than 5 cm—2 in in length) hatch they have to dig themselves out of their deep nest in the sand before making their way as quickly as possible to the relative safety of the sea. During this short but fearful journey they may be preyed upon by certain birds, carnivorous mammals, large crabs, and so on, even before they reach the surf. Once in the water they are somewhat safer, but they still have another whole gamut of marine predators to contend with. Marine turtles lay large numbers of

The eggs of the Green Turtle, *Chelonia mydas*, were at one time harvested in incredibly large numbers. In 1936, over 3,000,000 were taken! Photo by R. T. Zappalorti.

eggs for the simple reason that nature does not expect many of them to survive; but under natural conditions (that is without the technically "unfair" predation of modern humans) it is so organized that enough do survive to secure the continuing existance of the species.

Some countries sport what are known as "turtle ranches", a good example being the Cayman Islands. Here, the eggs are transported to safe incubati on sites or, alternatively, the hatchlings are collected as they hatch. The young turtles are then reared in large saltwater pools until they are large enough to be released into the ocean with a much greater chance of survival than if they were still hatchlings. A certain percentage of the turtles are kept for commercial gain and, of course, to finance the projects. The estimated survival rate of all natural hatchlings is just 2%, but with the releases from turtle ranches this is probably increased at least tenfold.

Species in the family include the Loggerhead Turtle, *Caretta caretta*, that has a genus all to itself. It is so named because of its broad head. Probably the hardiest of the marine turtles, they have been found as far north as the coast of Scotland and as far south as the River Plate in Argentina. Nesting on sub-tropical or temperate beaches, their 120-150 eggs take about 50 days to hatch. Fully grown, they are the largest species in the family, often growing to a meter in length (3.25 ft) and weighing up to 204 kg (450 lb). There are some unconfirmed reports of weights in excess of 511 kg (1125 lb). Such large turtles have a reputation for being aggressive, and there are many seamens' tales about frightening experiences, including overturned boats and savage bites.

The Green Turtle, *Chelonia mydas*, is one of the best known sea turtles. Its oval shell is characterized by the

Facing page: The few inches this young Loggerhead Sea Turtle, *Caretta caretta*, measures now gives no indication as to the 3-foot carapace it should have as a mature adult. Photo by J. Visser.

smoothness of the horny plates, which are closely knit and do not overlap. In spite of its name, colors range from olive-green through brown to almost black. Growing to a length of 1.4 meters (4.5 ft) and a weight of 300 kg (675 lb) or more, they are large reptiles. Adults are largely herbivorous, feeding on species of sea grass that grow in shallow tropical waters. Circumtropical in distribution but highly nomadic, they often breed at sites 2000 km (1250 miles) away from their feeding grounds. The Green Turtle was originally the favorite species used by European chefs in their famous turtle soups, so much in fact that the German name for the species is *Suppenschildkroete* (Soup Turtle). The only other species in the genus is the Flatback Turtle, *C. depressa*, found only in the waters off N. and N.E.

Australia, and is not migratory. Similar to the Green Turtle, it grows a little larger and remains mainly carnivorous throughout its life.

Another genus with a single species contains the Hawksbill Turtle, *Eretmochelys imbricata*, named after its narrow, hooked beak. Growing to just about 90 cm (35 in), specimens weighing over 100 kg (225 lb) are scarce. Found in the Atlantic and Indo-Pacific oceans, it has thick, rough, and often overlapping carapace plates which were (and still are in some places) much prized as the "tortoiseshell" material. When ground and polished they produce a beautiful, translucent, multi-colored material much in demand for the manufacture of ornaments and trinkets.

The genus *Lepidochelys* contains two species, the Atlantic or Kemp's Ridley Turtle, *L. kempii*, and the

Fortunately for the sea turtles, there are quite a large number of societies that dedicate their energies to sea turtle preservation. Photo of *Chelonia mydas* by R. T. Zappalorti.

Pacific or Olive Ridley Turtle, *L. olivacea*. As the common names imply, the former is native to the Atlantic, the latter to the Pacific oceans. Smallest of the sea turtles, the maximum length is about 75 cm (30 in). Both species are largely carnivorous. The eggs and the flesh of both species are edible but the Kemp's Turtle in particular is extremely endangered as a species.

FAMILY CHELYDRIDAE

There are just two species in this family, each in a separate genus, both of which occur in North America, and one reaching as far south as Ecuador. Both species are really unsuitable for the home terrarium, as they grow to a large size and can remain dangerous. In spite of this, young specimens make extremely interesting

Note in the lower half of this Alligator Snapping Turtle's (*Macroclemys temminckii*) jaw the pink, worm-like appendage it uses to lure its prey. Photo by W. P. Mara.

Although not often bred specifically for the herp hobby, newborn Snapping Turtles, *Chelydra serpentina*, make acceptable pets. Photo by R. T. Zappalorti.

inmates for the aquarium, and if you live in the right area you can re-release them into the wild when they get too big (however, on no account should any species be released in an area to which it is not native—this could lead to an environmental disaster).

The Common Snapping Turtle, *Chelydra serpentina*, is a ferocious species that, if pulled out of the water, will viciously attack anything that approaches it. Its sharp-edged jaws can inflict serious bites, even from small specimens, so handle them with extreme care! It is a primitive-looking beast, with a rough, almost horny shell, a long, crested tail, and a large head that it cannot withdraw under its carapace. Though reaching little more than 45 cm (18 in) in length, it can reach a weight of almost 35 kg (80 lb). It is uniformly drab brown in color, and often masked with a growth of algae. Found in the whole eastern half of the USA and south through Central America to Ecuador, it favors muddy, well-vegetated, fresh, and occasionally brackish, waters. It is highly aquatic and swims very well. It likes to bury itself under the mud in shallow water, with just its eyes and nostrils exposed and ready to lunge at any unsuspecting animal that comes into range. Meals include fish, amphibians, reptiles, birds, small mammals, invertebrates, and some vegetation. In captivity it should be supplied with a large aquarium with water warmed to at least 25°C (77°F). Feed on a variety of animal material, plus some greens (lettuce, spinach, dendelion, etc.). Adult specimens are best kept in large indoor or outdoor pools. In the USA, the main nesting season is in June, when up to 80 eggs are laid in a flask-shaped cavity about 20 cm (8 in) deep and often some distance from the water. Hatchlings often overwinter in the nest. Females can retain viable sperm for several seasons.

The Alligator Snapping Turtle, *Macroclemys temminckii*, is so named after its ferocious manner and habit of snapping up its prey. If anything, this species is even more bizarre than the Common Snapper. It is one of the largest of all freshwater turtles and carapace lengths of over 60 cm and a record weight of 99.5 kg (219 lbs.) have been recorded. It is similar in

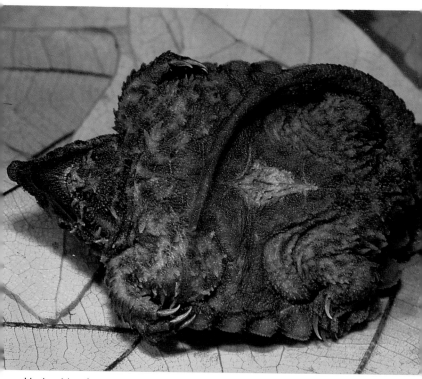

Underside of a neonatal Alligator Snapping Turtle, *Macroclemys temminckii*. Note the light area where the yolk sac was. Photo by R. D. Bartlett.

general appearance and color to the Common Snapper, but the head and the hooked jaw are larger. In a large specimen, the power of these sharp-edged jaws is so great that human fingers (or toes) could be sheared off with no problem at all, so be careful! Perhaps the most amazing feature of this animal is the worm-like appendage to its tongue that it uses to lure unsuspecting fish into its cavernous mouth before dispatching them into its gullet with a mighty gulp. The appendage looks amazingly like an earthworm, pink to red in color, even with segments of a "head" and "tail". Near its center it joins the tongue with a narrow bridge of tissue. To catch fish, the turtle lays on the river bed with its mouth open and wiggles its "worm"! This species occurs only in the USA and ranges from Illinois and Michigan to central Texas and eastward to the Florida panhandle. It prefers deeper waters in rivers and lakes, occasionally entering brackish water. It requires similar captive treatment to that described for the Common Snapper. Only nesting females normally venture onto land, where they excavate a flask-shaped nest near the water's edge. Nesting time is April to June and 10-50 spherical eggs are laid.

FAMILY DERMATEMYDIDAE

The family contains only a single genus and species, the Central American River Turtle, *Dermatemys mawii*, which inhabits rivers and lakes on the eastern side of Central America from Vera Cruz in Mexico, south to Honduras. The family is a primitive one which formerly had many species and is probably in the ancestry of the Emydidae, a successful, more recent family. Growing to a maximum 61 cm (24 in), it has a flattish, streamlined shell, and strongly webbed feet. The color is uniformly grayish to gray-brown. The head is dark greenish, and in the male the back part of the head has a reddish brown patch. The relatively small head has an upturned tubular snout. Not often available or

The Central American River Turtle, *Dermatemys mawi*, is the only surviving member of a very old family, Dermochelyidae. Photo by Peter Pritchard.

indeed suitable as a pet since it requires a large amount of heated swimming space. Juveniles are omnivorous, becoming progressively more herbivorous with age, feeding on aquatic vegetation, fallen leaves, and fruits. In the wet season, from September to November, clutches of up to 25 eggs are laid on banks of watercourses and covered with decaying vegetation.

FAMILY DERMOCHELYIDAE

Containing a single genus and species, this is another marine turtle that is never likely to be kept by the amateur enthusiast. However, the Leatherback Sea Turtle, *Dermochelys coriacea*, is interesting in being the largest of all turtles, and with the possible exception of the Saltwater Crocodile, *Crocodylus porosus*, would be a candidate for the heaviest reptile as well. Growing to a length of 185 cm (6 ft) and weighing up to 680 kg (1500 lbs) it is indeed a formidable creature. It is pan-tropical in distribution, occasionally venturing into temperate and even sub-arctic seas. The adult's carapace is leathery in texture with seven prominent ridges, and the scutes are reduced to small, bony platelets set at intervals in the skin. The color is uniformly blackish above, paler beneath. It feeds largely on jellyfish and crustaceans and nests on remote tropical beaches laying its 90 or so eggs in a hole at least one meter (3 ft) deep.

FAMILY EMYDIDAE

The largest of all chelonian families, containing about 85 species in 31 genera. Usually regarded as pond and river turtles, though some species are aquatic to varying degrees. Normally

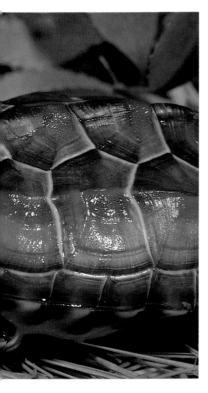

At one time, Reeves's Turtle, *Chinemys reevesi*, was hardly known to herp hobbyists. Now, its popularity is suddenly growing. Photo by J. Visser.

divided by most workers into two subfamilies, Batagurinae and Emydinae, the first comprising species of tropical and sub-tropical Asia and the stripe-necked species of North Africa and Europe plus the neo-tropical wood turtles of

tropical America; the second comprising the river turtles and sliders of N. America to Argentina, plus the European Pond Tortoise of Europe, N. Africa, and W. Asia. The family includes many species of turtles popular in the terrarium. The following is a selection of species:

Reeves's Turtle, *Chinemys reevesi*, is one of a genus containing three species native to Southeast Asia. Reeves Turtle is a small species reaching just 12.5 cm (5 in) carapace length. The elongated carapace, with three strong keels, is uniformly brown. There is a number of yellow to whitish stripes on the head and neck. Native to central and eastern China, Japan, and Korea, this species is one of the most frequently available Asian turtles. It is very hardy and usually does well in captivity; it may be kept outdoors in suitable climates. It is almost wholly carnivorous, feeding on a variety of animal material.

The Florida Red-bellied Turtle, *Pseudemys nelsoni*, is an attractive species that reaches an overall length of 35 cm (14 in). The carapace is highly arched and black with reddish markings. The plastron is usually a uniform reddish color. It has two tooth-like projections at the edge of the front of the upper jaw. It inhabits creeks, ponds, lakes, and swamps in peninsular Florida, where it is active all year and may often be seen basking on logs or mats of floating debris. Its breeding season is midsummer. In captivity it requires a large, heated aqua-terrarium or indoor pond. It may be kept outdoors during the summer only in cooler

areas. Adults become largely herbivorous with age, feeding on a variety of aquatic plants.

The Painted Turtle, *Chrysemys picta*, is a very attractive and popular member of the genus. It is a small species, rarely growing to more than 20 cm (8 in) in length. The carapace is usually dark brown and marked with bright red, especially on the marginal scutes. The head and neck are striped in yellow and there are red stripes on the limbs. Beneath, it is mainly creamy yellow. The most widespread turtle in North America, there are several subspecies ranging from British Columbia and Oregon to Nova Scotia and south to Oklahoma, Georgia, and Louisiana. It

Facing page: This photo should give you some indication as to how the Redbelly Turtle, *Pseudemys rubriventris*, got its name. Photo by K. T. Nemuras.

nests in May to July, laying up to 20 eggs. Young specimens are mainly carnivorous, becoming more herbivorous as they mature.

The Pond Slider, *Pseudemys scripta*, is a very popular species which has a wide range in the southeastern corner of the USA and south to Brazil. Colors are a wide range of greens and yellows, often striped and marbled together. A large female may reach 30 cm (12 in) in length. There are several subspecies, the most well known being the Red-eared Slider, *P. s. elegans*, that was formerly bred in turtle farms in large numbers and the hatchlings exported to many parts of the world. Its red or orange ear marking makes it easy to identify and it is one of the easier turtles to keep once reared past the baby stage. Its requirements are standard and the young are quite carnivorous, becoming more omnivorous as they mature.

It is quite easy to distinguish the sexes of adults as the male is smaller than the female, has a distinctly longer tail, and extremely long claws on the forelimbs; these are used to stroke the female's face during courtship procedures. Sliders are fond of basking and may often be seen on a suitable site stacked up one upon another. Though young specimens are suitable for the aqua-terrarium it is recommended that adults are kept in indoor or outdoor ponds with facilities to bask. Sandy areas should be provided for egg-laying. The nominate subspecies, the Yellow-bellied Slider, *P. s. scripta*, lacks the red ear markings but has generally

Facing page: The Sliders, *Pseudemys scripta*, have always been very popular with turtle enthusiasts. They are generally very attractive and quite adaptable to captive life. Photo by K. T. Nemuras.

more yellow in the overall pattern, while another, the Big Bend Slider, *P. s. gaigae*, has a large, black-bordered orange spot on the side of the head and a smaller orange spot behind the eye. Pond sliders breed in March to June and nest in June and July laying 2-3 clutches of 5-25 eggs, each about 37 mm (1 3/8 in) long. In the wild the 10 cm-deep nest cavity often may be some distance from the water.

Other species requiring similar care include the River Cooter, *P. concinna*; the Cooter, *P. floridana*; and the Red-bellied Turtle, *P. rubriventris*.

The Spotted Turtle, *Clemmys guttata*, is an attractive small species that grows to just 12.5 cm (5 in) in length. The carapace is smooth and black, usually with a scattering of round yellow spots. It also has yellow and reddish spots on its head and limbs. The plastron is cream-colored,

with large black markings along the edges. The male has brown eyes and a tan chin, while the female has orange eyes and a yellow chin. It occurs in the USA from southern Maine along the Atlantic coastal plain to northern Florida and extends inland as far as northeastern Illinois in the north, crossing into Canada along parts of the border. Inhabiting shallow, highly vegetated marshy areas the female digs her shallow nest and deposits 2-8 eggs in June. The hatchlings may emerge in fall or sometimes overwinter in the nest. This species is well-suited to a pond in an outdoor enclosure and should breed readily given suitable conditions. It is mainly carnivorous and will feed on a variety of meat, carrion, and invertebrates.

The Wood Turtle, *Clemmys insculpta*, grows to about 25 cm (10 in) in length and has shallow, pyramid-shaped carapace

Spotted Turtles, *Clemmys guttata*, are among the most charming and rewarding chelonians a keeper could ever hope to have. Photo by W. P. Mara.

scutes, mainly brown in color. The underside usually is yellow with black markings along the edges. The neck and forelimbs are often reddish orange. A very hardy species, it ranges from Nova Scotia south to northern Virginia and inland as far as northeastern Iowa and eastern Minnesota. It prefers areas in and around cool streams in deciduous

It is a shame that the Wood Turtle, *Clemmys insculpta*, is growing scarcer and scarcer everyday. It is an excellent captive. Photo by W. P. Mara.

woodland, though it may also occur in suitable cleared agricultural areas and will hunt terrestrially for worms and other invertebrates in damp weather. It nests in May and June, the female laying 2-18 eggs. Hatchlings often spend their first winter in the nest. It is an adept climber and has been known to scale a 6 ft wire link fence, a point that should be taken into consideration when planning its accommodation! It is best kept in a large outdoor enclosure with a shallow pond and facilities to bask and burrow. Feed on an omnivorous diet. Other species in the genus

Clemmys include the Western Pond Turtle, *C. marmorata*; and the Bog Turtle, *C. muhlenbergii*, an extremely rare, strictly northeastern North American species that has recently been placed on the CITES Endangered List.

The Amboina Box Turtle, *Cuora amboinensis*, is a member of a genus containing about five species of semi-aquatic Southeast Asian turtles with similar habits to the American box turtles but perhaps preferring it a bit wetter and warmer. Native to Indo-China and the Malayan-Indonesian Archipelago to the Philippines, all species of the genus inhabit swampy areas and sometimes turn up in the rice paddies. The Amboina Box Turtle is a very popular and colorful

Note the egg tooth on this newborn Wood Turtle, *Clemmys insculpta*. Note also the "soft" quality of the shell and the as of yet undeveloped sculpturing on the scutes. Photo by R. T. Zappalorti.

subject for the warm aqua-terrarium. The highly domed carapace is usually a dark greenish brown and there are vivid yellow stripes on each side of the head. The plastron is much lighter in color. Temperature should remain in the range of 25-32°C (77-90°F) and it should have a shallow pool for bathing. Mainly carnivorous, it will feed on a variety of animal material. Other species in the genus requiring similar care include the Yellow-margined Box Turtle, *C. flavomarginata*; the White-fronted Box Turtle, *C. galbinifrons* (this species is perhaps the most terrestrial of the group); and the Three-keeled Box Turtle, *C. trifasciata*. All species in the genus will benefit from a regular ration of natural sunlight or broad spectrum artificial light.

The Chicken Turtle, *Deirochelys reticularia*, has an extremely long neck for an emydid turtle. The carapace length is a maximum of 25 cm (10 in) but the head and neck may be almost as long again. The neck is striped in green, yellow, and black. The carapace is brownish, finely wrinkled, and with a pale reticulate pattern. There are yellow stripes on the forelimbs. It inhabits densely vegetated shallow lakes, ponds, and ditches in the south eastern coastal plain areas of the USA from Virginia to Florida and Texas. There are three subspecies within the range. In southern Florida the Chicken Turtle breeds throughout the year, laying several clutches of 4-16 eggs in a hole about 10 cm (4 in) deep. At one time the Chicken Turtle was eaten as a delicacy. It is a shy species but will quickly settle into captivity given a heated terrarium or pond. It is omnivorous, becoming more herbivorous with age.

Blanding's Turtle, *Emydoidea blandingii*, is

Blanding's Turtle, *Emydoidea blandingii*, is not often seen in the hobby, but should be considered when it is available. It makes a superb pet. Photo by R. T. Zappalorti.

the only member of its genus. Reaching 25 cm (10 in) in length, it is one of the hardiest of all turtles and has been seen swimming under the ice in its native habitat, which includes large bodies of water in the Great Lakes region of southern Canada and the USA. It was previously included with the European Pond Turtle in the genus *Emys* but research showed

The European Pond Turtle, *Emys orbicularis*, is a hardy carnivore that seems to do well in captivity but does not often breed in domestic conditions. Photo by Peter Pritchard.

it to warrant its own genus. The smooth carapace is blackish with profuse small brownish spots, The hinged plastron is yellowish; the head and limbs brownish, but the chin and throat are bright yellow. It nests in June to July laying about eight eggs. Suitable for an outdoor pond, it feeds on a variety of animal matter.

The European Pond Turtle, *Emys orbicularis*, is one of the few chelonians native to central Europe and was once a popular terrarium animal on that continent. However, the species is becoming increasingly rare, probably due to climatic change, habitat destruction (land drainage), pollution, and formerly, collection for food. It is now protected by law in most countries where it occurs, but some specimens are still bred in captivity and may occasionally become available. The wild range includes most of central and southern Europe, northern Africa, and the Middle East, though it must be stressed that in many locations it is extremely rare. It is a small species, rarely growing in excess of 20 cm (8 in). It may be black or dark brown, usually with a light pattern of spots and streaks. The head is usually covered with yellowish spots. It

Rarely seen in the hobby, the Notched or Leaf Turtle, *Geoemyda spengleri*, is the last remaining species of a genus that was at one time very large. Photo by R. D. Bartlett.

prefers habitats with still or slow-moving water and much vegetation. In captivity it requires a large aqua-terrarium or, preferably, an outdoor enclosure and pond. It lays up to 12 eggs in the summer months. In captivity the eggs are best incubated artificially since northern summers are often not warm enough or long enough for full development. This species is almost entirely carnivorous, feeding on a variety of vertebrates, fish, and carrion.

The Notched or Leaf Turtle, *Geoemyda spengleri*, is a singular species with no subspecies. Native to Southeast Asia, it lives mainly in tropical forests where it is often quite some distance from water. Reaching a carapace length of 15 cm (16 in), it is a somewhat flattened species and rather plain brown in color, with the posterior marginal scutes deeply

notched. In captivity it requires a warm, humid, aqua-terrarium. Feed on a variety of animal and vegetable material.

The Common Map Turtle, *Graptemys geographica*, like other map turtles, gets its common name from the

Geoemyda spengleri is native to the tropical forests of Southeast Asia and can sometimes be found quite a long way from water. Photo by R. D. Bartlett.

ground color is olive green with a pattern of yellow lines which may be obscured in aged specimens. The skin of the head and limbs is greenish with narrow yellow stripes. There is a conspicuous yellow spot behind the eye. Mainly carnivorous in all stages, adult females are capable of crushing the shells of relatively large molluscs. It nests during May to July, laying up to 15 eggs. Found in eastern central USA from the Great Lakes region south to Alabama and Tennessee, it inhabits vegetated, slow-moving rivers and lakes. They may sometimes be seen basking in large stacks, but as they are extremely shy they quickly drop into the water if disturbed.

pattern of yellowish lines in its carapace scutes that are reminiscent of the contour lines on a map. When fully grown, the male reaches a maximum length of just 15 cm (6 in), the female considerably larger at almost twice the length. The

The False Map Turtle, *Graptemys pseudogeographica*, is similar in size to the preceding species, also with the adult male being only half the length of the female. Coloration is also similar, though perhaps duller, and there is a variation among the three subspecies. Once very abundant in the systems of the Ohio, Mississippi, and Missouri rivers, its numbers have been drastically reduced, probably as a result of pollution and over-collecting (it is still

Facing page: Once a False Map Turtle, *Graptemys pseudogeographica*, has begun eating in captivity, a keeper will find it to be quite voracious. Photo by Isabelle Francais. **Below:** Occasionally, a False Map Turtle, *Graptemys pseudogeographica*, will have to be "sparked" into an eating routine by being given earthworms and crickets rather than commercially produced foods. Photo by W. P. Mara.

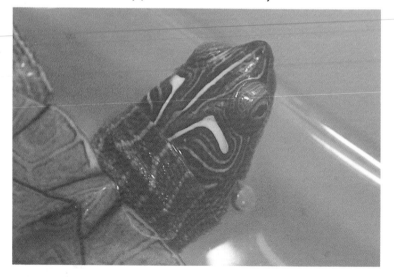

Albinism seems to be much more common in snakes than in turtles, but every now and then an example rises to the surface. Photo of an albino Spiny Turtle, *Heosemys grandis*, by R. D. Bartlett.

considered a delicacy by some people). Some of the other species in the genus include the Yellow-blotched Sawback, *G. flavimaculata*; the Mississipi Map Turtle, *G. kohnii*; the Black-knobbed Sawback, *G. nigrinoda*; and the Alabama Map Turtle, *G. pulchra*.

An interesting and bizarre group of Southeast Asian turtles are to be found in the genus *Heosemys*, which inhabit smaller watercourses in the tropical and montane rainforests of Indo-China and the Malaysian Archipelago.

Of the five species, the best known seems to be the Spiny Turtle, *H. grandis*, which is also the largest in the genus, growing to 40 cm (16 in) in carapace length. It makes an exceptionally good pet, becoming quite tame and trusting. One drawback is its eventual size, which is too large for the average home aqua-terrarium.

However, it can be kept successfully in a heated indoor enclosure with a pool. It is mainly dark brown to black above, lighter brown with dark streaks below. It has a ridge along the center of the carapace and sharp spines on the marginal laminae that are particularly prominent in juveniles. The Cog-wheel Turtle, *H. spinosa*, is even more spectacular although smaller at 20 cm (8 in). It has an almost circular carapace, set off with very sharp extensions to the rear of both the costal and marginal scutes making it resemble a cog-wheel. It is reddish brown above and yellowish below, with the scutes of the plastron marked with radiating black lines. It does quite well in the heated aqua-terrarium and is a prized species if it can be obtained. It is more or less omnivorous, feeding on a variety of animal and plant material.

Hobbyists who have had the opportunity to own a Spiny Turtle, *Heosemys grandis*, say they are first-rate pets. Photo by Mervin R. Roberts.

The so-called roof turtles, *Kachuga*, of India and northern Indo-China are named because of their high-domed shells and the separate vertebral keels on the carapace that make them resemble the roof of an oriental building. Of the six species, the Indian Roof Turtle, *K. tecta*, is the best known and most color[...]

though none of the species can be regarded as common in captivity. As the species are all subject to CITES controls in most countries, it is only a continuation of captive-bred stocks which will make them available. *K. tecta* occurs in the rivers of Pakistan and northern India where it is extremely aquatic and makes quickly for deep water if disturbed while sunbathing. The brown carapace is a maximum of 23 cm (9 in) in length and marked with red or orange on the marginals and along the dorsal ridge. The neck is striped with narrow yellow lines and there may be a red patch just behind the eye. They are omnivorous and most will consume a large amount of green food; the droppings e thus copious

f Turtle, *Kachuga*
nivorous species
ladesh south of
portedly a very
Photo by K. T.
Nemuras.

so hygiene is most important. A very efficient filtration or, preferably, water exchange system is required. Water should be heated to 25-27°C (77-81°F). Data on captive breeding seems to be very sparse. There are said to be two subspecies, *K. t. tecta* and *K. t. tentoria*, though some workers now regard the latter as a separate species.

The Snail-eating Turtle, *Malayemys subtrijuga*, is a small, tropical rainforest species (20 cm—8 in) from Indo-China, Malaysia, and Indonesia. The shell is reddish brown, with yellow marginals marked in black. There are white stripes on the head and neck. Largely carnivorous and

After years of being regarded as nothing more than a source of meat, the Diamondback Terrapins, *Malaclemys terrapin*, are now starting to grow in popularity as hobby animals. Their one major flaw: a hunger for raw fish. Photo by K. T. Nemuras.

specializing in snails, this species is said to be a difficult captive.

The Diamondback Terrapin, *Malaclemys terrapin*, is the only species in its genus, but many subspecies have been described. At the turn of the century the meat of this species was highly prized in gourmet restaurants and as a consequence its numbers were greatly reduced. However, commercial farming of the species seems to have helped preserve it. Nowadays it is rarely used for culinary purposes. The female (25 cm—10 in) grows much larger than the male (15 cm—6 in). The carapace is light brown to gray or black while the skin of the head and limbs is pale gray with a scattering of black spots. The lips are often orange or white. It occurs in salt marsh estuaries and tidal flats along almost the whole of the US eastern seaboard and the Gulf Coast as far as southern Texas. The breeding season is April to May in the southern part of its range, June or July in the north. It lays 4-18 eggs in sandy cavities 10-20 cm (4-8 in) deep. In captivity it must have access to saltwater otherwise skin diseases are likely to ensue. This can be accomplished by adding a teaspoonful of salt (the kosher variety is good) to each gallon of water. As it is almost entirely carnivorous it will take a variety of animal foods including lean meat, worms, crustaceans, and snails, and especially loves raw fish. Enthusiasts living near the seashore can collect a variety of littoral invertebrates for them.

The Caspian or Stripe-necked Terrapin, *Mauremys caspica*, is the only other freshwater turtle species found in Europe next to the European Pond Turtle, *E. orbicularis*. Its range includes Iberia and the Balkans, North Africa, and

Although many hobbyists prefer to ignore the Diamondback Terrapins due to their need for brackish water, the truth is this type of requirement is actually very easy to replicate. Photo by William B. Allen, Jr.

southwestern Asia, where it inhabits rivers, streams, and lakes. It rarely exceeds 25 cm (10 in) in length. The color is usually a mottled gray-green to brown. There is a number of yellow and/or white stripes along the neck. In captivity it is best kept in an outdoor enclosure with a pool. Mostly carnivorous, it will feed on a variety of meat, fish, and invertebrates. The Japanese Turtle, *M. japonica*, is a small species barely reaching 15 cm (6 in) in length. It makes an excellent subject for the terrarium if it can be acquired, but it is not often available. It occurs naturally in Japan from Tokyo southwards. It requires a heated aqua-terrarium.

The Chinese Strip-necked Turtle, *Ocadia sinensis*, is a hardy Asian species that seems to do better if kept outdoors during the warmer months. Photo by Peter Pritchard.

The Mexican Wood Turtle, *Rhinoclemmys pulcherrima*, has only recently begun being captive-bred in any great numbers. Photo by W. P. Mara.

The Chinese Striped Turtle, *Ocadia sinensis*, is a popular and small species from southwestern China and Indo-China. The three-keeled carapace reaches a maximum length of 40 cm (16 in) but it is usually smaller. The color of the shell is brownish olive and the head and neck are attractively marked in yellow and black stripes. It makes a good captive and may be kept outside during the summer months. Feed on a variety of vegetable and animal material.

Tropical wood turtles of the genus *Rhinoclemmys*

The attractive head stripes on the Mexican Wood Turtle, *Rhinoclemmys pulcherrima*, are one of this animal's most endearing features. Photo by W. P. Mara.

include a little more than half a dozen. They are colorful and attractive turtles that will do well in the tropical aqua-terrarium given the right conditions. They are native to tropical Central and South America where they inhabit a variety of wetland situations. The Mexican Wood Turtle, *R. pulcherrima*, found from Mexico to Costa Rica, is probably the best known of the genus. Reaching a carapace length of 20 cm (8 in), it is chestnut brown to blackish, marked with red. It has a number of narrow, black-bordered, yellow or red stripes on the head and neck and similar colorful markings on the limbs. All members of the genus are primarily carnivorous, taking a variety of vertebrate and invertebrate food and a

The Fat-headed Turtle, *Siebenrockiella crassicollis*, is a carnivorous species that needs its tank heated to at least 75°F. Photo by R. D. Bartlett.

small amount of vegetable material.

The Fat-headed Turtle, *Siebenrockiella crassicollis*, is the only member of its genus and comes from Indo-China and the Indonesian Archipelago. Maximum carapace length is about 20 cm (8 in). It has a single dorsal keel on its blackish brown carapace. It is mainly aquatic and carnivorous. Provide a heated aqua-terrarium with water temperature around 26°C (79°F). Feed on a variety of animal material.

The Eastern Box Turtle, *Terrapene carolina*, is one of the most beloved of all North American chelonians. Found in eastern, southern, and central USA, usually in moist, wooded areas, flood plains, and marshy meadows. The species varies tremendously both from individual to individual and according to geographical range, and several subspecies have been described. The maximum length is 20 cm (8 in). They are mainly terrestrial but they prefer damp areas and often overwinter in mud. Being omnivorous, they subsist on a variety of insects, molluscs, and some carrion, as well as fruits, leaves, and fungi, including some of the latter that are poisonous to humans. Captive specimens will thrive on a diet of soft fruits (strawberries, raspberries, blackcurrents, tomatoes, pears, etc.), greens, and mushrooms, plus earthworms, snails, and lean, raw meat, plus a regular vitamin/mineral supplement.

Most Eastern Box Turtles are attractively colored with yellow, orange, and dark brown stripes and blotches on the shell, limbs, and head. The carapace is highly domed and the hinged plastron allows the lower shell to close tightly against the carapace. Their habits are similar to those

Box Turtles have always been very popular in the herp hobby, and many have become the basis for various forms of herpetological artwork. Photo by W. P. Mara.

of land tortoises, though they can swim well if the occasion arises. Box turtles may be kept in indoor or outdoor terraria and should do well if they have access to sunlight and fresh air in the summer. Box tortoises are notoriously long-lived and there are records of specimens over 100 years old. Occasionally, box turtles are turtles bred in captivity. Wild specimens

Although *Terrapene carolina triunguis* is known as the Three-toed Box Turtle, the name is somewhat misleading since some specimens have four. Photo by R. T. Zappalorti.

nest June to July and lay 3-10 eggs in a 7-10 cm (3-4 in) deep cavity. Hatchlings frequently spend the winter in the nest before emerging the following spring. Females are able to store viable sperm for several years and often produce fertile eggs up to five years after mating.

T. ornata, is the other species in the genus. It is

similar in shape to the preceding species, but even smaller (15 cm/6 in maximum). It is dark brown to black with radiating light brown to yellow lines on the shell, and similarly colored spots on the head and limbs. Occurring in the more arid areas of central southern USA and into Mexico, this species inhabits open prairies and woodlands in arid terrain often near waterways. It is primarily insectivorous in

A very young Ornate Box Turtle, *Terrapene ornata ornata*. Photo by R. D. Bartlett.

the wild but in captivity will soon adjust to a similar diet as described for *T. carolina*.

FAMILY KINOSTERNIDAE

There are 23 species in four genera in this family comprising the American mud and musk turtles that range from eastern Canada, through USA and Central America, and as far south as Argentina. The family is sometimes divided into two subfamilies, Kinosterninae (comprising the genera *Kinosternon* and *Sternotherus*) and Staurotypinae (comprising the genera *Claudius* and *Staurotypus*. Some workers prefer to regard the latter as a distinct family (Staurotypidae—Mexican Mud Turtles).

The Narrow-bridged Musk Turtle, *Claudius angustatus*, from eastern Mexico to Belize, is the only species in its genus. Growing to just 10 cm (4 in) in carapace length, this feisty little turtle has an extraordinarily large head for its size. There are three low ridges on the carapace and the cross-shaped plastron is relatively small. It is uniformly brown in color. It should be kept in a large aquarium with a water depth of 20-30 cm (8-12 in) and a temperature of 25-28°C (77-82°F). Feeds on a variety of animal food but may occasionally take soft fruit. Only a small land area (plastic container full of damp sand) is required. Breeds in the summer, laying 10-35 eggs in a shallow cavity.

The Eastern Mud Turtle, *Kinosternon subrubrum*, is a member of a genus containing about 15 species native to North, Central, and South America. Most of the mud turtles are capable of emitting a foul smell from

Facing page: The plastral scutes of the Eastern Mud Turtle, *Kinosternon subrubrum subrubrum*. Photo by K. T. Nemuras.

their cloacal glands. This is usually done when the turtle thinks it is in danger, so you will have to put up with a certain "holding" of your nose when handling your specimens until they become tame enough to stop doing it! *K. subrubrum* is one of the best known in the genus and was formerly a frequent import for European enthusiasts. It is found over much of the southern USA and is still quite common in most parts of its range. It prefers shallow, swampy areas and spends much of its time foraging about in bog vegetation. A small species, rarely longer than 12.5 cm (5 in), it has a smooth carapace that is usually uniformly reddish brown to olive in color. Like other members of the genus, the plastron is double-hinged

Albino Red-eared Sliders, *Pseudemys scripta elegans*, are somewhat common in today's hobby, but albino Flattened Musk Turtles, *Sternotherus depressus*, like the one shown here, are not. Photo by R. D. Bartlett.

Most of the Mud Turtle species make fairly hardy captives, but they usually do not care to be handled. Photo of *Kinosternon baurii "palmarum"* by R. D. Bartlett.

so that both head and tail can be totally closed off. The males have a blunt spine on the tip of the tail. Some mud turtles are bad-tempered and can give quite a nasty nip with their sharp jaws. Largely carnivorous, they will take a variety of vertebrate and invertebrate food. They require a medium-sized aqua-terrarium with basically equal amounts of land and water. They usually breed in mid-March to May and nest in June to October (several clutches in warmer parts of the range), laying 2-6 eggs in a shallow cavity, sometimes under decaying vegetation or in the burrow

The Mississippi Mud Turtle, *Kinosternon subrubrum hippocrepis*, can be easily identified by the two light yellow lines on its head. Photo by R. D. Bartlett.

of a small animal.

The Striped Mud Turtle, *K. baurii*, is another small but more colorful species, found in southern Georgia and peninsular Florida. The light brown carapace is marked with three light stripes and the head is striped and spotted with yellow. This is a fairly terrestrial species, requiring minimum water. Care otherwise as for *K. subrubrum*.

The Yellow Mud Turtle, *K. flavescens*, occurs from Illinois southwest to Arizona and northeastern Mexico. It is a larger species, reaching 17 cm (7 in) in length. The carapace is usually light brown, with the head and neck yellowish. This also requires similar care as described for *K. subrubrum*.

The Scorpion Mud Turtle, *K. scorpioides*, is the largest in the genus, reaching 20 cm (8 in). It is a widely distributed species with several subspecies ranging from western and southeastern Mexico to northern Argentina. The

Although not often seen in private collections, the Yellow Mud Turtle, *Kinosternon flavescens*, nevertheless makes a fine captive. Photo by Dr. Herbert R. Axelrod.

carapace is usually reddish brown and the head is spotted with red or yellow. It requires heated accommodation (water temperature minimum 25°C/77°F).

The Giant Musk Turtle, *Staurotypus triporcatus*, is found from eastern Mexico to Belize and Guatemala. It is a relatively large and pugnaceous species, growing to 40 cm (16 in) in carapace length. The carapace has three ridges, and the plastron is small and cross-shaped. The head is relatively large. The color is a mixture of light and dark brown, sometimes with yellowish spots on the head and neck. Largely aquatic, feeding on a variety of animal material. It requires a large aquarium or indoor pool with water temperatures around 25°C (77°F). A small land area with sand is required for egg-laying. The other member of the genus is the Pacific Coast Giant Musk Turtle, *S. salvinii*.

The Stinkpot Turtle, *Sternotherus odoratus*, lives up to its unfortunate but appropriate common and scientific names. It is the best known of the musk turtles in a genus that contains a number of species limited to eastern USA and renowned for its habit of releasing a foul-smelling fluid from the musk glands under the carapace. The Stinkpot is a small species, reaching 13 cm (5.5 in) in total length. It occurs in all of the eastern states of the USA, over to central Texas and north to southern Wisconsin. As well as emitting musk, it is quite pugnaceous and will attempt to bite if handled. It has a smooth, rounded carapace that is usually yellowish brown in color. There are two white stripes on each side of the head. The head is relatively large, and unlike members of the genus *Kinosternon*, the plastron is hinged at the

The Stinkpot, *Sternotherus odoratus*, gets its name from the foul smell it produces to ward off aggressors. Photo by Peter Pritchard.

rear only. Care is as described for *Kinosternon*, though *Sternotherus* is generally more aquatic. The breeding season is from February to June, depending on the climatic range. Courtship and mating take place below water. The female lays 2-10 eggs in a shallow cavity often excavated under the roots of a waterside tree or in a muskrat burrow. The young hatch in 9-12 weeks. Other species in the genus include the Razorback Musk Turtle, *S. carinatus*; the Flattened Musk Turtle, *S. depressus*; and the Loggerhead Musk Turtle, *S. minor*.

FAMILY TESTUDINIDAE

This family contains about 40 species of land tortoises in ten genera distributed in tropical and sub-tropical areas on all major land masses except Australia and Antarctica. All are completely terrestrial. Most have highly arched or domed shells, and the limbs are unwebbed. The rear limbs are often columnar and elephantine, while the forelimbs are flattened and heavily scaled. The family includes the great island species of Galapagos and Aldabra as well as some popular smaller varieties.

Horsfield's or the Four-toed Tortoise, *Testudo horsfieldii*, is the only member of the subgenus *Agrionemys* and hails from the drier areas of southern central Asia, including Turkmenistan, Uzbekistan, Iran, Afghanistan, and Pakistan, inhabiting the steppes and semi-deserts. With a maximum carapace length of 25 cm (10 in), the shell is relatively flat and round. The forelimbs are four-clawed and strongly adapted for digging deep tunnels. Frequently active for only four months of the year, April to July, as estivation during the dry period often extends into a further period of winter hibernation. In damper climates, captive specimens are best kept indoors as they are unable to tolerate periods of cool humidity. A tortoise table with a basking lamp is ideal. It is mainly herbivorous and should be provided with a range of fruit and green food, supplemented with minced lean meat (ox heart), canned dog or cat food, and a regular vitamin/mineral supplement.

The Radiated Tortoise, *Geochelone (Asterochelys) radiata*, comes from the island of Madagascar and although it is very attractive and does fairly well in

In some places where the Radiated Tortoise, *Geochelone radiata*, occurs, it is highly regarded by locals and treated with much respect. Photo by Jeff Wines.

captivity it is an endangered species that is supposed to be strictly protected in the wild, though it is said to be regarded as a delicacy by the natives! Only occasional captive-bred specimens may be available, and it seems that the species may only survive as a captive species. The relatively high-domed carapace reaches 40 cm (16 in) in length and is dark brown, marked with yellow-buff radiations. It is confined to the savannah regions of southwestern Madagascar. The famous Tui Malila, a tortoise reputedly presented to the Queen of Tonga by British explorer Captain Cook in 1777 and which died in 1966, was said to be a Radiated Tortoise. It requires a dry terrarium in captivity with facilities for basking. Feed on a variety of vegetable material, some animal matter, and regular mineral/vitamin supplements.

The only other species in the subgenus is the closely related *Geochelone (Asterochelys) yniphora*, another endangered species. It occurs in the tropical forests of northwestern Madagascar. The carapace color is sandy, with dark flecks. Requires similar conditions to *G. (A.) radiata*, but can perhaps tolerate a somewhat higher humidity.

The Red-footed Tortoise, *Geochelone (Chelonoidis) carbonaria*, is a very attractive and popular species from the tropical forests of northern South America. The elongated carapace reaches a maximum length of 50 cm (20 in) and is pinched near the center, forming a distinctive hourglass shape. The carapace color is almost black, with the centers of the scutes being yellow-buff, tinged with red. The marginals are also tinged with red. There are yellow and orange markings on the head, and the limbs are adorned with a sprinkling of conspicuous orange-red scales. It is a forest shade-loving tortoise and feeds on a variety of vegetable matter, plus some carrion. It is especially fond

Facing page: For the hobbyist, the Radiated Tortoise, *Geochelone radiata*, is an "easy captive" and can be bred with little trouble. Photo by R. D. Bartlett.

The Yellow-legged Tortoise, *Geochelone denticulata*, is a native of South American rainforest regions and the largest tortoise species of the continental mainland. Photo by Peter Pritchard.

of soft, ripe fruits. It requires a large, humid, heated terrarium or, more preferably, a tortoise room. Feed on a variety of fruits and greens, plus some animal material and regular vitamin supplements. Provide the occasional lukewarm bath.

The Argentinian Tortoise, *Geochelone (Chelonoidis) chilensis*, is a small species from the arid regions of central South America. It reaches just 22 cm (9 in) in total carapace length. The carapace is brownish yellow, with the individual scutes bordered in black. It requires a dry terrarium and may be kept outdoors in warm, dry periods. Feed as for *G. (C.) carbonaria*.

The Yellow-legged or Jaboty Tortoise, *Geochelone (Chelonoidis) denticulata*, is similar to the Red-legged Tortoise but grows to a length of 70 cm (28 in), though the average is much shorter. The leg scales are yellow in color rather than red. This is another rainforest inhabitant that likes the warmth and the shade. Feeding and care as for *G. (C.) carbonaria*.

Galapagos Giant Tortoises, *Geochelone nigra*, are unlikely to be kept as pets by the average home enthusiast, but some of the subspecies are kept and bred regularly in zoological collections. The Galapagos Islands are situated in the Pacific Ocean about 1050

The Bowsprit Tortoise, *Chersina angulata*, is a hardy desert species that occurs in southern Africa. Photo by Paul Freed.

km (660 miles) west of Ecuador. They have been the subject of much discussion ever since Charles Darwin wrote about his visit there in his *Voyage of the Beagle* in 1835. Darwin studied the differences and similarities of animals from the various islands, and this helped him formulate his controversial (at that time) theory of evolution.

The giant tortoises were particularly interesting in this respect, and each island was found to possess its own subspecies, adapted to life on that particular island. About ten of these subspecies still exist, but several have become extinct since their discovery (and most probably due to it). Today there are two major groups among the subspecies, the saddleback type and the domeshell type. These arose from the method of obtaining food. The saddlebacks live on arid islands where they continually have to reach high up for vegetation, while the domeshells live in damper areas where vegetation can be grazed directly from the ground. They range in length from 90-120 cm (36-44 in) and in weight from 40-570 kg (90-1280 lbs).

The Bowsprit Tortoise, *Chersina angulata*, from southern Africa, has an elongated, domed carapace reaching 25 cm (10 in) in length. A tortoise of the savannah and semi-desert, it gets its common name from the characteristic projecting gular plate. The color is yellowish, marked with dark brown. The plastron is often tinged with pink. It is largely herbivorous. It requires a dry terrarium with facilities for basking and a temperature reduction at night.

The Star Tortoise, *Geochelone elegans*, at one time was one of the most frequently available exotic

The starlike pattern that gives the Starred Tortoise, *Geochelone elegans*, its common name is an effective camouflage when hiding in tufts of tall, dry grass. Photo by F. Broderick.

land tortoises; captive-bred specimens should still be occasionally available. Native to India and Sri Lanka, they reach a maximum carapace length of 25 cm (10 in). The carapace is highly domed and each of the vertebral and pleural scutes cone-shaped. Basic coloration is black with a yellow-buff star pattern on each scute, giving it an attractive appearance. It is a predominantly fruit-eating species, but will take some meat as well. This species requires heated indoor accommodations though it may be kept outside in the warmer summer months. It is very susceptible to cold and drafts, but is fond of a regular lukewarm bath. It is endangered in many of its native habitats.

The Leopard Tortoise, *Geochelone pardalis*, is a native of the drier parts of central and southern Africa. With a total length of 70 cm (28 in) it has an attractive black and yellow-buff carapace. It is popular as a pet if it can be obtained. It requires similar care to that described for the Star Tortoise. The other two species in this genus also requiring similar care are the Burmese Tortoise, *G. platynota* (Burma, western Thailand), and the Spurred Tortoise, *G. sulcata* (Senegal to Eritrea).

The gopher tortoises, *Gopherus*, are a hardy American species that at one time were recommended as pets and appeared on the pet market in America and Europe. They are now largely protected in most states, so any prospective collector of wild specimens should thus make himself aware of the legal regulations before collecting any species. The eastern American Gopher Tortoise, *G. polyphemus*, was once very abundant in the southeastern states, including the Carolinas, Georgia, Alabama, Mississippi, and Florida. Adult specimens occasionally reach 35 cm (14 in) maximum carapace length. The carapace color is dark brown to black with a lighter blotchy pattern. The head and limbs are also blackish. The Gopher Tortoise is an adept burrower and it has shovel-like forelimbs to help it construct tunnels up to 12 meters (40 ft) long with a sleeping chamber at the end up to 3 meters (10 ft) below the surface. Gopher

Facing page: The Leopard Tortoise, *Geochelone pardalis*, is a fairly popular herbivore that would appreciate a small amount of crushed bone meal in its daily diet. Photo by Isabelle Francais.

As a newborn, the Gopher Tortoise, *Gopherus polyphemus*, has yellowish scutes outlined in thick black. As an adult, this outlining will be almost bluish. Photo by Peter Pritchard.

Tortoise burrows are often used as refuges for other animals, including armadillos, gophers, rabbits, raccoons, rats, indigo snakes, and lizards. Even rattlesnakes are said to live peaceably with the other inhabitants when they are at home. Gopher tortoises were once used by people as food items and were dragged from their burrows by hooks on the end of long, flexible poles.

The flesh of the tortoise is called "low ham." Declining numbers of Gopher Tortoises have led to the collection of them from the wild to be largely forbidden. Gopher Tortoises are mainly herbivorous and captive specimens should be fed on a variety of green food and fruits. Wild specimens are active mainly at night, spending the daylight hours in their burrows. In captivity they may become semi-diurnal but should be provided with facilities for burrowing. Because they are considered difficult captives, most American herpetologists do not consider them suitable as pets for novices. Other species in the genus include the Desert Tortoise, *G. agassizii* (southwestern USA, northwestern Mexico); the Texas Tortoise, *G. berlandieri* (southern Texas and northeastern Mexico)

Native to the southeastern corner of the United States, the Gopher Tortoise, *Gopherus polyphemus*, is generally protected by local laws and seldom encountered in private collections. Photo by R. T. Zappalorti.

In its native land, the Parrot-beaked Tortoise, *Homopus areolatus*, occasionally gets attacked by predatory birds. Photo by J. Visser.

and the Bolson Tortoise, *G. flavomarginatus* (northern Mexico).

The Parrot-beaked Tortoise, *Homopus areolatus*, with its characteristic hooked beak, is one of the smallest of all land tortoises, with a maximum carapace length of 13 cm (5 in). Native to the southeastern areas of Cape Province, this species has a rather flattened carapace with dark-bordered brownish scutes. It also has four claws on its forelimbs. It is herbivorous, feeding on a specialist diet of succulent semi-desert plants in its native habitat. It is rarely seen in captive situations and is probably not easily kept. There are three other species in the genus: Boulenger's Tortoise, *H. boulengeri*; the Karoo Tortoise, *H. femoralis*; and the Spotted Tortoise, *H. signatus*.

The Elongate Tortoise, *Indotestudo elongata*, is so named after its typically elongated carapace, which has a maximum length of 30 cm (12 in). The carapace is light yellowish brown and

there are dark patches in each scute. The head is characteristically pale yellow to whitish. It occurs in eastern India and through Indo-China to the Malaysian Archipelago. It will do quite well in an indoor heated terrarium with médium humidity. Feed on a variety of vegetable material with a little meat and a regular vitamin/mineral supplement.

Bell's Hinge-backed Tortoise, *Kinixys belliana*, is one of three bizarre, closely related species of land tortoises occurring in tropical Africa. The carapace is elongated, with a characteristic hinge of cartilagenous material toward the rear that probably evolved as a means of protecting the rear end from predators. The maximum carapace length is about 25 cm (10 in). This species is the best known and probably best suited for captivity in the genus. Since it occurs in dry savannah to semi-desert in the wild it should be provided with a warm (temperature reduction at night), dry terrarium. Feed on a variety of fruits and greenery, plus meat, and a regular vitamin/mineral supplements. The Forest Hinge-back Tortoise, *K.*

The bizarre-looking Pancake Tortoise, *Malacochersus tornieri*, is becoming very popular with turtle enthusiasts. Photo by John Coborn.

erosa, is somewhat larger (33 cm—13 in) and requires more humid conditions, as does Home's Hinge-backed Tortoise, *K. homeana*.

The Pancake Tortoise, *Malacochersus tornieri*, is an extreme example of tortoisedom. It is very popular as a bizarre pet—if it can be obtained. It is unusual in having a very flat appearance, almost as if it had been run over by an automobile. The maximum carapace length is about 17 cm (7 in). Occurring in eastern Africa, it lives in rocky outcrops at medium altitudes where it is able to hide in crevices as protection from predators. Since the shell is moderately soft and pliable, it is able to inflate the body and jam itself in between the rocks, making it extremely difficult to remove. It is a relatively active species and quite speedy for a tortoise, quickly scuttling for cover when disturbed. Unfortunately, it has been declared an endangered species due to loss of habitat, plus over-collection for food and for the pet trade. It had been regularly bred in captivity, though it rarely lays more than two eggs per clutch.

In England I kept a pair of Pancake Tortoises for many years, and for much

In the wild, the Pancake Tortoise, *Malacochersus tornieri*, spends quite a bit of its time climbing rocks and can even be found under them. Photo by Robert S. Simmons.

of this time I gave them free run of the house (which had winter floor heating, allowing the tortoises to decide how warm they wanted to be by seeking out the parts that were or were not heated). They liked to live under the sideboard or a bookshelf but quickly emerged at feeding time. Though mating activity was frequently observed, eggs were never laid, although a laying trough was provided. Eventually the female escaped via the back door one day and in spite of intense searching she was never seen again, probably perishing in the cold, damp winter. The male lived for a further two years before finally contracting a chill and we were unable to save him (he had been with us for nine years and was an adult when we obtained him). Pancake tortoises are mostly vegetarian and I found mine to be very fussy regarding what they ate; lettuce was the favorite food, followed by tomato, cucumber and banana. Anything else offered was usually ignored, so it was important to dust what they would take with a vitamin/mineral supplement about twice per week. Captive specimens can also be kept satisfactorily in a spacious, heated terrarium with facilities to climb and hide. Daytime temperature to 23°C (73°F), with a basking lamp for extra heat if required. At night, allow the terrarium to drop to room temperature.

The Burmese Mountain Tortoise, *Manouria emys*, is native to Assam, India, and eastwards through Indo-China and the Malaysian/Indonesian Region. One of the larger Asian tortoises, it grows to a maximum of 60 cm (23 in) carapace length. It is generally a fairly dull brown color. Living in tropical forests, it is omnivorous, feeding on a variety of invertebrates, small vertebrates, and

The Burmese Mountain Tortoise, *Manouria emys*, is a dull-colored omnivore from the tropical forests of Assam,India east to the Malaysian/Indonesian region. Photo by Peter Pritchard.

carrion, as well as fruit and green food. It requires a large, humid terrarium with The temperature maintained at 30°C (86°F) in the daytime, and about 23°C (73°F) at night. Feed on a variety of vegetable and animal matter. A smaller, attractively colored relative, *M. impressa*, reaching a maximum length

The eggs of the Aldabra Giant Tortoise, *Geochelone gigantea*, are white, spherical, and about the size of tennis balls! Photo by Jeff Wines.

of 30 cm (12 in), occurs in Indo-China and the Malayan Peninsula. The carapace is decorated in black and orange-brown, while the head is yellow. Care as for *M. emys*.

The Aldabra Giant tortoise, *Geochelone (Megalochelys) gigantea*, is the largest of modern land tortoises, with a maximum carapace length of 140 cm (56 in) and a total weight of up to 240 kg (540 lb). It is not likely to be kept as a pet in the home, but is still a frequent exhibit in zoological gardens. Living on the Indian Ocean island of Aldabra, an outpost of the Seychelles (Zil Eloigne Sesel), its isolation and protection ensure its relative abundance. Proper management in the future should hold this magnificent reptile for future generations. In the wild state it feeds largely on the sparse available vegetation, and there is a conflict between the amount it can eat and the time it can spend out of the shade. Shade trees are sparse, and if the tortoise grazes too far away from them it can perish in the hot sun from overheating. Consequently there are areas of lush, edible vegetation on parts of the island that are not available

The Aldabra Giant Tortoise, *Geochelone gigantea*, is famous for its remarkable longevity. Some are known to have lived over 125 years. Photo by Peter Pritchard.

For many hobbyists, the smaller the pet, the more manageable it will be. The Geometric Tortoise, *Psammobates geometricus*, for example, almost never exceeds 6 inches. Photo by Peter Pritchard.

to the tortoises. In addition to vegetation it is also an opportunistic eater of carrion.

The Aldabra Giant Tortoise is uniformly brown in color. In captivity it requires a large, heated enclosure with access to the outdoors during warmer periods. It will feed on almost anything offered to it, and I have known zoo specimens to take pizza, hamburgers, and even ice cream (although none of these items are advised!).

The Geometric Tortoise, *Psammobates geometricus*, is one of three small, endangered tortoise species native to southern Africa. Reaching 25 cm (10 in) carapace length, the Geometric Tortoise is the largest and best known in the genus. The name comes from the geometric, black and yellow-buff, radial pattern on the carapace scutes. It is a difficult captive due to its specialized diet of native grasses.

The Egyptian Tortoise, *Testudo (Pseudotestudo) kleinmanni*, is a small species with a maximum carapace length of 13.5 cm (5 in). The domed carapace is yellowish, the individual scutes being dark-bordered. It occurs in scrubland areas of eastern Libya, through Egypt to southern Israel. This is another specialized feeder that does not normally do well in captivity and, indeed, is rarely available.

The Spider Tortoise, *Pyxis arachnoides*, is native to the savannah regions of southwestern Madagascar (Malagasy Republic). A small species reaching just

The Spider Tortoise, *Pyxis arachnoides*, is not often seen in captivity, but supposedly makes a willing and reliable pet. Photo by R. D. Bartlett.

One of the most popular tortoise pets of all time, at least in Europe, is the Greek Tortoise, *Testudo graeca*. It is a hardy, attractive animal, and reportedly quite amenable to domestic surroundings. Photo by Isabelle Francais.

12 cm (4.5) in total carapace length. The carapace is dark brown and decorated with a web-like pattern of yellow-buff, hence its common and specific names. In the wild this species estivates in a burrow during the dry season and feeds on a variety of vegetable and animal matter. It makes a good terrarium inmate if given climatic considerations, e.g., high daytime temperature (30°C—86°F) cooled to 20°C (68°F) at night, wet and dry seasons, and facilities to burrow. Females lay 2-3 eggs per clutch. The closely related Flat-backed Spider Tortoise, *P. planicauda*, from western Madagascar is rarely imported and little is known about its habits.

The Greek Tortoise, *Testudo graeca*, is one of three species of European tortoise that have long been popular as pets, though unfortunately it is only in recent times that any

thought has been given to their scientific welfare. *T. graeca*, in spite of its specific and common names, is not a native of Greece but of southwestern Spain and much of North Africa. Subspecies occur in Israel and Turkey, through to central Iran. The moderately domed carapace has a maximum length of about 30 cm (12 in) and it is easily distinguished from the other *Testudo* species by the presence of a bony spur on the back of each thigh. The carapace color is a mixture of brown and buff to yellowish, and younger specimens are noticeably brighter in color. Sex determination is quite simple in that males have a readily recognizable concave plastron, while that

Facing page: Shown here is a stack of very popular tortoise pets: on the bottom, the Leopard Tortoise, *Geochelone pardalis*, and on top of it, the Greek Tortoise, *Testudo graeca*. Photo by Isabelle Francais.

of the female is quite flat. In the wild state, this species lives in fairly arid regions, feeding on a variety of vegetation plus occasional carrion.

Until the late 1970's, thousands of these and other *Testudo* species were imported into the cities of northern Europe from southern Europe, North Africa, and Asia Minor. Imports usually arrived in spring, and pet shops often remained well-stocked until about September. I remember seeing wholesalers offering such tortoises in quantities of, 100-10,000 at a time; no wonder these reptiles began to become more and more difficult to find! Fortunately, conservationists eventually persuaded governments to restrict exports and imports and to monitor licensed possession. Presently many *Testudo* are bred in reasonable numbers in captivity and it is hoped that this will eventually satisfy demand for these fascinating creatures.

Statistics have shown that of the millions of imports in the past, only 10% or less were likely to survive their first year in an alien climate, due mainly to ignorance of their requirements by the keepers. With proper care, these tortoises make rewarding and entertaining pets that can reach a ripe old age of 100 years or more.

Hermann's Tortoise, *Testudo hermanni*, is another popular species that was formerly collected in large numbers for the pet trade. It is similar in appearance to *T. graeca* but a little smaller (25 cm—10 in) and with a single spine on the tail tip instead of spines on the thighs. Habits are similar and hybridization has been known in wild specimens (where ranges overlap) and in captive stock. *T.*

There was a time when thousands of Hermann's Tortoises, *Testudo hermanni*, were collected solely for the pet industry. Now, captive breeding helps cut down much of this activity. Photo by H. Reinhard.

hermanni ranges from the Balkan Peninsula to Italy and the Iberian Peninsula.

The Margined Tortoise, *Testudo marginata*, is a scarcer species that occurs only in Greece from Mount Olympus southwards, plus a few small Aegean Islands (and Sardinia and parts of the Italian mainland, where it was probably introduced). The maximum carapace length is 35 cm (14 in). Mature specimens are very distinctive, with the rear part of the carapace strongly flared. The color is dark brown to black, each scute having a yellow or orange patch. Scarcer in captivity than the two foregoing species but prized as a pet when available, habits and care are similar to *T. graeca*.

FAMILY TRIONYCHIDAE

This distinctive family contains the softshell turtles, of which there are 22 species in six genera, often divided into two subfamilies comprising the typical softshells of the genera *Chitra*, *Pelochelys*, and *Trionyx* (Trionychinae), and the so-called flapshells of the genera *Cyclanorbis*, *Cycloderma*, and *Lissemys* (Cyclanorbinae). These flapshells have a flap-like extension on either side of

the rear of the plastron, used to shield the hind limbs from attack. Occurring in the warmer parts of North America, Africa, and Asia, the softshells can hardly be mistaken for any other group of chelonians as the typical bony shell of the carapace is reduced and the scutes are replaced with a soft, leathery skin that in some species is nicely patterned and colored. All softshells are aquatic, and the snout elongated almost like a proboscis so that the animal can easily breathe without surfacing. They usually select a spot to rest in the mud in the shallows so that the water surface can be just reached with the snout. Having paddle-like, three-clawed limbs, they are adept swimmers. All species are carnivorous, feeding mainly on fish which they catch by the ambush method, but also on other animals, and any carrion that they happen to come across. They are capable of striking at great speed with their razor-sharp jaws and often, in the case of large fish being grabbed, they content themselves with a "bite-sized chunk", which accounts for the many scars seen on fish caught by anglers in softshell territory.

Softshells seldom become tame in the sort of way that they can be stroked and petted, but they tend to become fearless and capable of regarding any object placed near them as an item for the menu—and this includes fingers.

The Indian River Turtle, *Chitra indica*, is one of the largest members of the family Trionychidae, reaching a carapace length of almost 4 feet. Photo by Dr. Sherman A. Minton.

In some of its native areas, the Senegal Softshell Turtle, *Cyclanorbis senegalensis*, is considered a food item rather than a pet. Photo by R. D. Bartlett.

Needless to say, like snappers, mud turtles, and musk turtles, they are not suitable as beginners' pets. In view of their general pugnacity they are best kept singly, only introducing sexes when a mating response is required.

The Indian River Turtle or Narrow-headed Softshell, *Chitra indica*, is, at the time of writing, the only member of its genus and unlikely to be kept as a pet in view of its large size (up to 115 cm—45 in carapace length). However, as it is one of the largest softshells, a brief description will not go amiss. Found in the river systems of India and Indo-China, it is infamous for its unsavory activities, which include boat sinking and biting toes off! It has a relatively long neck for a softshell, and a small head with the eyes set very close to the short proboscis. There is an attractive pattern of dark, wavy lines on the light brown carapace and there are light stripes on the top of the head. It

The Senegal Softshell Turtle, *Cyclanorbis senegalensis*, is a reasonably small species with a maximum carapace length of 30 cm (12 in). It occurs in the larger rivers from Sudan to West Africa. It is widely used as a food item by the natives. The carapace is olive to dark green with a paler margin. It requires a large aquarium with a gravel substrate about 10 cm (4 in) deep and a water depth about 15 cm (6 in) above this, so that the turtle can conceal itself but still reach the water surface with its snout. Since the droppings of softshells are fluid and copious, an efficient filter and water exchange system is required. Temperature of the water should range in the vicinity of 24-28°C (75-82°F). Feed on strips of meat and fish, plus whole (dead) baby mice. Another interesting member of the genus is the Nubian Softshell, *C. elegans*, which

feeds primarily on fish. Only very young specimens are suitable for the home terrarium, but then there is the problem of disposal once the animals are too big. It should be hoped that zoos will always have space for surplus specimens!

The Indian Flapshell Turtle, *Lissemys punctata*, is considered the most primitive of the softshells and, as you can see here, is quite beautifully marked. Photo by Robert S. Simmons.

grows to 60 cm (24 in) and occurs from the Sudan to Nigeria.

Aubrey's Softshell Turtle, *Cycloderma aubryi*, is a medium-sized softshell from West Africa, occurring especially in the Congo region. Reaching a maximum length of about 35 cm (14 in), its color is mainly yellowish brown with a few darker blotches. There are dark lines on the head, and juveniles have a dark dorsal line on the carapace which fades with age. Care is as described for

Cyclanorbis senegalensis. The only other member of this genus is the Bridled Softshell, *C. frenatum*, which is found in lakes and pools in eastern Africa from Tanzania to Mozambique.

The Indian Flapshell Turtle, *Lissemys punctata*, the most primitive softshell, is one of only two members of its genus and occurs throughout India and Sri Lanka. Adults average 20 cm (8 in) in carapace length and have a relatively domed carapace that is olive green with round lemon yellow spots while the plastron (that has large posterior side flaps) is mainly yellow. The head also has round yellow spots. Being small and attractive, it is a prized terrarium species but usually difficult to obtain. It requires a heated aquarium

Although it makes an excellent captive and is reportedly fairly easy to breed, the Indian Flapshell Turtle, *Lissemys punctata*, is difficult to obtain commercially.

with shallow water and a fairly deep gravel substrate. It is totally carnivorous and should be provided with a variety of animal material. In the wild, this species often lives in temporary waters that dry up in the dry season. Estivation is therefore seen as an aid to promoting a breeding response. In captivity, a few weeks during the summer, give no water, just a damp substrate deep enough for the turtle to conceal itself. This will compromise a period of estivation. On returning to the water it is probable that a breeding response will occur if you have a true pair. Needless to say, a "land" section (a plastic container full of damp sand) must be provided for egg-laying.

The Giant Softshell Turtle, *Pelochelys bibroni*, vies for the distinction of being the largest softshell along with *C. indica*. Specimens up to 130 cm (51 in) in length have been reported. In view of their size, they are unlikely to be kept by the home enthusiast. They live in a wide variety of watery habitats from India to Indo-China and Indonesia to New Guinea, often venturing into brackish, and even salt, waters, a fact that could explain their wide island distribution.

The Florida Softshell Turtle, *Trionyx ferox*, is one of three N. American softshells and the one most likely to be a captive. Occurring naturally in peninsular Florida and southern Georgia, including the Okeefenokee Swamp. Growing to about 45 cm (18 in) (female) and 30 cm (12 in) (male) in carapace length, the color is mainly dark brown, marbled with olive and buff. It requires a large aquarium with a deep substrate of coarse sand and water shallow enough for the turtle to reach the surface with its snout. Feed on a variety of animal

As adults, softshells can be very temperamental and thus slightly dangerous, but as newborns they are generally quite calm and well-contained. Photo by Guy van den Bossche.

Only one species of *Trionyx*, *Trionyx triunguis*, occurs in Africa. In some circles it is known as the Nile Softshell Turtle. Photo by R. D. Bartlett.

material. Other North American species in this genus are the Smooth Softshell, *T. muticus*, and the Spiny Softshell, *T. spiniferus*, named for the rubbery "spines" on its carapace.

The Chinese Softshell Turtle, *Trionyx sinensis*, occurs in the Amur river system of eastern Russia, through China to Vietnam. Also in Japan and Taiwan, it has been successfully introduced into Hawaii, originally as a source of food! It is a small species, with a maximum carapace length of 25 cm (10 in). It typically has a grayish olive carapace bearing indistinct black markings. The young are more attractively marked with rounded, light-edged black spots.

The Malayan Softshell Turtle, *Trionyx subplanus*, is another small species reaching just 25 cm (10 in) carapace length. It ranges through Burma, Thailand, Malaysia, Indonesia, and the Philippines. The carapace is somewhat elongated. It has a relatively long neck and

The Smooth Softshell Turtle, *Trionyx mutica*, is a common North American species occasionally seen in captivity. Photo of a juvenile specimen by Robert S. Simmons.

large head. The color is mainly dark brown, with light spots on the head and a few darker blotches on the carapace. This species has sometimes been placed in a separate genus, *Dogania*. Other Asian members of the genus include the Ganges Softshell, *T. gangeticus*, numbers of which are kept in a large artificial reservoir at Puri in India and are fed and protected by their Islamic worshipers; and the Peacock Softshell, *T. hurum*, of Eastern India, young specimens having four conspicuous "eye" markings on the carapace.

The only member of both its family and genus, the Big-headed Turtle, *Platysternon megacephalum*, gets its name from a head so large it cannot be withdrawn into the shell. Photo by K. T. Nemuras.

The Nile Softshell Turtle, *Trionyx triunguis*, is found over the African continent in most of the larger river systems and also extends into Syria. Growing to about 90 cm (36 in) carapace length, it is dark brown to olive with numerous lighter spots.

FAMILY PLATYSTERNIDAE

With a single species in a single genus, the Big-headed Turtle, *Platysternon megacephalum*, is an interesting and bizarre species quite suitable for the cool aqua-terrarium. It is native to the shallow, cool mountain streams of southern Burma through Thailand and Indo-China to southern China. It has a maximum carapace length of 20 cm (8 in). It has a very large head that cannot be withdrawn under the carapace. It has a formidable, hook-shaped beak and an uncertain temper, which means it must be handled with respect. It has a long, scaly tail, reminiscent of the North American snapping turtles. The head, limbs,

Of all the longnecks, perhaps the best known to hobbyists is the Australian Snake-necked Turtle, *Chelodina longicollis*. Photo by H. Budde.

documented though it is said to lay just two eggs at a time.

SUBORDER PLEURODIRA

FAMILY CHELIDAE

Contains about 37 species in nine genera. Confined to tropical and temperate South America, Australia, and New Guinea. As with all members of the suborder Pleurodira, the head retracts into the shell in a horizontal rather than a vertical plane. All have rather long necks but some are excessively long.

The Australian Snake-necked Turtle, *Chelodina longicollis*, is one of the best known "longnecks" and is frequently kept as a pet in Australia, where it occurs

and shell are black, marked with brown speckles. It requires an aqua-terrarium with shallow water and rocks over which it will climb. Maintain temperature around 23°C (73°F), cooler at night. May be kept in an outside enclosure during summer months. Feeds mainly on molluscs and will take as many snails as you can find. However, the diet can be supplemented with other animal material. Its breeding habits are poorly

Most hobbyists report that the Australian Snake-necked Turtle, *Chelodina longicollis*, does well in captivity, eventually taking food right from the keeper's hand. Photo by H. Budde.

in rivers, lakes, and billabongs, right along the eastern quarter of the continent. It is also famous for being the first Australian turtle discovered, having been collected on Captain Cook's voyage of discovery in 1770. As its name implies, it has a neck almost as long as the carapace that has a maximum of about 25 cm (10 in). It is a rather plainly colored reptile, the carapace, head, neck, and limbs all being uniformly olive-brown to almost black while the plastron is yellowish. Hatchlings, however (which are just 3 cm (1.25 in) in length), have an orange stripe along each side of the lower jaw and neck and orange spots on the plastron. The eyes are

yellow with round pupils, giving the animal a piercing expression. It is a very popular terrarium inmate and makes an entertaining pet, quickly taming and learning to "beg" for food by standing almost upright in the water and stretching out its long neck in a most comical manner. It will take most animal food, including fish and raw meat. It requires a large aqua-terrarium with facilities to bask and a water temperature of 24-27°C

Perhaps the most unusual-looking turtle of all is the Matamata, *Chelus fimbriatus*. This probably explains much of the popularity it has enjoyed over the years. Not only do Matamatas inspire much intrigue, they also make excellent captives. Photo by R. D. Bartlett.

(75-81°F). A few other species in the genus with similar habits are the Broad-shelled River Turtle, *C. expansa*, the New Guinea Long-necked Turtle, *C. novaeguineae*, the Oblong Turtle, *C. oblonga*, the Northern Snake-necked Turtle, *C. rugosa*, and the Flat-shelled Turtle, *C. steindachneri*.

The Matamata, *Chelus fimbriatus*, is perhaps the most bizarre of all the world's chelonians. Inhabiting slow-moving and stagnant waters in tropical South America, the Matamata lurks among the mud and decaying vegetation at the bottom, in perfect disguise with strange warts and appendages which resemble the dead leaves around it. When fish or other prey come close enough it suddenly opens its wide, cavernous mouth, dropping the the lower jaw and creating a strong water current that actually pulls the prey into its gullet. Growing to a length of 45 cm (18 in), the Matamata is mainly reddish brown with darker markings. The carapace is fairly flat, with three ridges. The head is broad and flat and the snout is proboscis-like. It requires a large, heated aquarium with shallow (20 cm—8 in) water and a deep substrate. Gravel and roots of treated driftwood supplied for the aquaria should be used for decoration rather than attempting to create a "natural" habitat with decaying vegetation, since this would create problems of hygiene. An adequate water exchange/filtration system is also highly recommended. Although this species prefers a diet of live fish and invertebrates, it will soon learn to take pieces of dead fish (complete with scales and bones) and meat under captive conditions.

The Saw-shelled Turtle,

The Matamata, *Chelus fimbriatus*, is a highly aquatic species that will sit on the floors of slow-moving South American waterways and patiently await its next meal. Photo by K. T. Nemuras.

Elseya latisternum, is a small turtle with only a moderately long neck. The maximum carapace length is 20 cm (8 in). The carapace is broadly oval with a serrated rear edge. Color is brown to dark brown above, whitish beneath. Juveniles usually have a yellow stripe along the neck, which is sometimes retained into adulthood. It occurs in rivers of eastern and northeastern Australia feeding on molluscs, crustaceans, and fish, and will take a varied animal diet in captivity. Breeding

The Murray River Turtle, *Emydura macquarrii*, is not offered on the commercial market with much frequency, which is probably no loss to hobbyists as it is reputedly quite nasty. Photo by Ken Lucas, Steinhart Aquarium.

season is during the southern summer (November to January) when the female lays 8-15 eggs in a shallow burrow. Other species in this genus include the Northern Snapping Turtle, *E. dentata*, and the New Guinea Snapper, *E. novaeguineae*.

The Murray River Turtle, *Emydura macquarrii*, is widely distributed throughout the Murray/Darling river system west of the Great Dividing Range in southeastern Australia. Unlike the snakenecks (*Chelodina*) that are fairly docile and friendly in captivity, members of this genus can be snappy and are capable of inflicting a painful bite. Maximum length of the carapace is about 32 cm plain brown to olive above, yellowish white beneath. The carapace is somewhat flattened and the neck is relatively short. This species is mainly carnivorous and will feed on a variety of animal foods. In the southern summer the female lays about 10 eggs in a cavity on a river bank. There are four other species in the genus, including the Brisbane Short-necked Turtle, *E. signata*, and Krefft's Turtle, *E. krefftii*.

The South American Snake-necked Turtles, *Hydromedusa maximiliani*, from southwestern Brazil, and *H. tectifera*, from southwestern Brazil, Paraguay, Uruguay and Argentina, are similar in appearance to *Chelodina*.

A species related to the Murray River Turtle but not known to have quite as bad a temper is the Brisbane Short-necked Turtle, *Emydura signata*. Photo by R. D. Bartlett.

The Twist-necked Turtle, *Platemys platycephala*, is a highly aquatic species in the wild, but the keeper should remember that it likes to spend time basking as well. Photo by Robert S. Simmons.

Growing to 25 cm (10 in), they have a neck of similar length. Fairly uniformly dull in coloration, they require similar captive requirements to *Chelodina*.

The Twist-necked Turtle, *Platemys platycephala*, is a small side-necked turtle from Guyana and Surinam, through northern Brazil to eastern Peru, with a maximum carapace length of 20 cm (8 in). It has a very flat shell and a relatively short neck. There are two ridges on the carapace, which are brown with a lighter edge. The plastron is dark brown with a yellowish edge and the top of the head is reddish to yellowish brown. It occurs in various bodies of water in the rainforest and is largely carnivorous. It should do well in a heated aqua-terrarium with the water temperature around 23°C (73°F) and facilities to bask under a heat lamp. Feed on a variety of animal material. There are three other species in the genus requiring similar care, *P. spixii* (Brazil), *P. pallidipectoris* (Chaco area of Argentina), and *P. radiolata* (Amazon Basin).

Newborn Helmeted Turtles, *Pelomedusa subrufa*, were once very common since the adults were available to breeders in large numbers. Photo by J. Visser.

Helmeted Turtles, *Pelomedusa subrufa*, will spend much of their captive time basking under heat lamps, if such lamps are provided. Photo by K. T. Nemuras.

FAMILY PELOMEDUSIDAE

Contains about 24 species in five genera occurring in Africa, Madagascar and South America.

The Helmeted Turtle, *Pelomedusa subrufa*, was formerly one of the most frequently available African turtles in pet shops. Found over most of Africa south of the Sahara and in Madagascar, this species has a maximum carapace length of about 25 cm (10 in). The shell is uniformly brown-olive with only faint variational markings. The head is broad and the limbs are well-developed. It is an excellent swimmer, but also likes to sunbathe on logs, sandy banks, or even on the backs of crocodiles and hippos! When watercourses dry up this species may

The Yellow-bellied Mud Turtle, *Pelusios castanoides*, is a native of Madagascar, southeastern Africa, and the Seychelle Islands. Photo by J. Visser.

travel some distance over land in search of more water. A good captive, specimens have survived for years in a small aqua-terrarium with facilities to bask (heat lamp). They will appreciate a natural sunbath in the warmer weather, so maybe you should place them outside in the summer months. Feed on a variety of animal material. It is the only member of its genus, but there are two well-defined

Most of the *Pelusios* turtles make fair pets, but obtaining one may be difficult. Photo of *Pelusios sinuatus* by J. Visser.

subspecies. *P. s. subrufa*, and *P. s. olivacea*.

African Mud Turtles, *Pelusios niger* and *P. subniger*, are probably the best known and most widespread of the eight or so species in the genus. Between them they occur over most of tropical and sub-tropical Africa south of the Sahara. All members of this genus have the front part of the plastron hinged so that the head and forelimbs can be concealed. Carapace length is 35-40 cm (14-16 in) and the color is mainly blackish with faint radiations on the carapace scutes. The head and limbs are usually yellowish brown. The general habits and care of these species are similar to that described for *Pelomedusa*.

The Yellow-spotted River Turtle, *Podocnemis unifilis*, is probably the best species for the terrarium out of the entire genus.

An attractive native of southern Africa, *Pelusios rhodesianus* was considered a subspecies of *P. castaneus* until around 1980. Photo by J. Visser.

Note the bright red head markings that give this Red-headed River Turtle, *Podocnemis erythrocephala*, its common name. This trait is already obvious even in newborn specimens. Photo by Robert S. Simmons.

Unfortunately, the size of an adult (45 cm—18 in) means it requires a lot of swimming space, although juvenile specimens, once tamed, make excellent and docile pets, showing none of the nervousness associated with the emydid turtles. This species has a semi-domed carapace, narrow at the front and broader at the rear, with a low dorsal ridge. It is primarily black

Calm temperament and a remarkable ability to adapt to captive life are two traits generally attributed to the *Podocnemis* species. Photo of *Podocnemis unifilis* by R. D. Bartlett.

At one time, the Yellow-spotted River Turtle, *Podocnemis unifilis*, enjoyed more popularity in the hobby than any other member of its genus. Now it is highly protected. Photo of 14 neonates by Harald Schultz.

in color, light gray beneath. The triangular head is also black but attractively marked with bright yellow spots. Front and hindlimbs are strongly clawed and webbed. It is omnivorous and will take a variety of green food as well as the usual animal material.

Shown here is the well-known Arrau River Turtle, *Podocnemis expansa*, a species that can attain a length of almost 3 feet. Photo by Harald Schultz.

Juveniles may be kept in a heated aqua-terrarium but larger specimens are better suited to a large, heated, indoor pool. Other species in the genus include the famous Arrau River Turtle, *P. expansa*, which grows to 80 cm (32 in) in length. Once very common in the river systems of the Amazon Basin, this species has been exploited by man to such an extent that it has declined dramatically and disappeared from many of its old haunts. The eggs were collected for food and for oil extraction. Attempts at providing protection for this and other turtle species have been only partially successful. However, due to the threatened status of most species in this genus, they are seldom available. This is a shame as there is

Once, many of the Arrau River Turtles, *Podocnemis expansa*, were collected for food. Photo by Harald Schultz.

a good chance that serious captive breeding programs could contribute to the conservation of the species, as conservation of the habitats seems to be almost an impossibility.

This man is collecting an Arrau River Turtle, *Podocnemis expansa*, so he can sell it for meat. Photo by Harald Schultz.

Bibliography

The following is a selection of books that will provide the reader with further information on turtles. All make interesting reading:

Cobb, Jo. (1987) A Complete Introduction To Turtles. T.F.H. Publications, Neptune, NJ.

Conant, Roger and Collins, Joseph T. (1991) A Field Guide to the Reptiles and Amphibians of Eastern and Central North America. Houghton Mifflin, Boston, MA.

Ernst, Carl H. and Barbour, Roger W. (1972) Turtles of the United States. University of Kentucky Press, Lexington, KY.

Freiberg, Marcos. (1981) Turtles of South America. T.F.H. Publications, Neptune, NJ.

Frye, Dr. Fredric L. (1991) Reptile Care, An Atlas of Diseases and Treatments. T.F.H. Publications, Neptune, NJ.

Jocher, Willy. (1973) Turtles for Home and Garden. T.F.H. Publications, Neptune, NJ.

Pritchard, Peter C. H. (1979) Encyclopedia of Turtles. T.F.H. Publications, Neptune N.J.

Zimmermann, Elke. (1986) Reptiles and Amphibians. T.F.H. Publications, Neptune, NJ.

Further information on turtles and their care may be obtained from the various local, state, and national turtle clubs or herpetological societies, who meet regularly and publish findings on all aspects of turtle studies as well as offer fellowship for all turtle enthusiasts.

Photo Index

Aldabra Giant Tortoise, **211**

Alligator Snapping Turtle, **86**, **142**, **145**

Arrau River Turtle, **250**, **251**, **252**

Australian Snake-necked Turtle, **232**, **233**

Big-headed Turtle, **230–231**

Blanding's Turtle, **26–27**, **159**

Bog Turtle, **8**, **83**

Bowsprit Tortoise, **197**

Box turtle, **181**

Brisbane Short-necked Turtle, **239**

Brown Roof Turtle, **170–171**

Burmese Mountain Tortoise, **209**

Caretta caretta, **139**

Carettochelys insculpta, **130**, **131**

Central American River Turtle, **147**

Chelodina longicollis, **36–37**, **232**, **233**

Chelonia mydas, **137**, **141**

Chelus fimbriatus, **234–235**, **237**

Chelydra serpentina, **123**, **143**

Chelydra serpentina osceola, **17**

Chelydra sp., **85**

Chersina angulata, **197**

Chinemys reevesi, **29**, **148–149**

Chinese Stripe-necked Turtle, **9**, **176**

Chitra indica, **221**

Chrysemys picta, **24**, **106**

Chrysemys picta marginata (two headed), **3**

Chrysemys picta picta, **15**

Clemmys guttata, **109**, **155**

Clemmys insculpta, **20**, **89**, **156**, **157**

Clemmys muhlenbergii, **8**, **83**

Crayfish, **72**

Cyclanorbis senegalensis, **222–223**

Dermatemys mawi, **147**

Diamondback Terrapin, **31**, **172–173**, **175**

Eastern Box Turtle, **35**

Eastern Mud Turtle, **185**

Eastern Painted Turtle, **15**

Eggs, of Aldabra Giant Tortoise, **210**

Emydoidea blandingii, **26–27**, **159**

Emydura macquarrii, **238**

Emydura signata, **239**

Emys orbicularis, **160**

Eretmochelys imbricata, **19**, **134**

European Pond Turtle, **160**

False Map Turtle, **164**, **165**

Fat-headed Turtle, **179**

Flattened Musk Turtle, **186**

Florida Redbelly Turtle, **82**

Florida Snapping Turtle, **17**

Fly River Turtle, **130**, **131**

Geochelone denticulata, **126–127**, **196**

Geochelone elegans, **199**

Geochelone gigantea, **211**

Geochelone pardalis, **128**, **201**, **217**

Geochelone radiata, **6**, **11**, **193**, **195**

Geometric Tortoise, **212**

Geomyda spengleri, **161**, **163**

Giant Mealworm Beetle, **74**

Gopher Tortoise, **202**, **203**

Gopher Tortoise (albino), **1**

Gopherus polyphemus, **202**, **203**

Gopherus agassizii, **1**

Graptemys pseudogeographica, **164**, **165**

Greek Tortoise, **214–215**, **217**

Green Turtle, **137**, **141**

Hawksbill Turtle, **19**, **134**

Helmeted Turtle, **241**, **242–243**

Heosemys grandis, **166–167**, **169**

Hermann's Tortoise, **23**, **219**

Homopus areolatus, **204–205**

Indian Flapshell Turtle, **224**, **225**

Indian River Turtle, **221**

Kachuga smithi, **170–171**

Kinixys belliana, **92**

Kinixys spekii, **93**

Kinosternon baurii "palmarum", **187**

Kinosternon flavescens, **189**

Kinosternon subrubrum hippocrepis, **188**

Kinosternon subrubrum subrubrum, **185**

Leaf Turtle, **161**, **163**

Leopard Tortoise, **201**, **217**

Lissemys punctata, **224**, **225**

Loggerhead Sea Turtle, **139**

Macrobrachium rosenbergii, **72**

Macroclemys temminckii, **142**, **145**

Malaclemys terrapin, **31**, **172–173**, **175**

Malaclemys terrapin terrapin, **96**

Malacochersus tornieri, **206**, **207**

Mandible, overgrown, **81**

Manouria emys, **209**

Matamata, **234–235**, **237**

Mexican Wood Turtle, **177**, **178**

Midland Painted Turtle (two-headed), **3**

Mississippi Mud Turtle, **188**

Murray River Turtle, **238**

Nile Softshell Turtle, **228**

Northern Diamondback Terrapin, **96**

Notched Turtle, **161**, **163**

Notochelys platynota, **10**

Ocadia sinensis, **9**, **176**

Ornate Box Turtle, **183**

Painted Turtle, **24**, **106**

Pancake Tortoise, **206**, **207**

Parrot-beaked Tortoise, **204–205**

Pelomedusa subrufa, **241**, **242–243**

Pelusios castanoides, **244**

Pelusios rhodesianus, **246**

Pelusios sinuatus, **245**

Pig-nosed Turtle, **130**, **131**
Pillbug, **73**
Platemys platycephala, **240**
Platysternon megacephalum, **230–231**
Podocnemis erythrocephala, **247**
Podocnemis expansa, **250**, **251**, **252**
Podocnemis sp., **117**
Podocnemis unifilis, **248**, **249**
Pool, outdoor, for turtles, 62
Porcellio scaber, **73**
Psammobates geometricus, **212**
Psammobates tentorius, **128**
Pseudemys cocinna suwanniensis, **30**
Pseudemys nelsoni, **82**
Pseudemys rubriventris, **79**, **91**, **151**
Pseudemys scripta, **153**
Pseudemys scripta elegans, **13**, **65**, **125**
Pyxis arachnoides, **213**
Radiated Tortoise, **6**, **11**, **193**, **195**
Red-eared Slider, **13**, **65**, **125**
Red-headed River Turtle, **247**
Redbelly Turtle, **79**, **91**, **151**
Reeves's Turtle, **29**, **148–149**
Rhinoclemmys pulcherrima, **177**, **178**
Senegal Softshell Turtle, **222–223**
Shrimp, **71**
Side-necked turtle, **117**
Siebenrockiella crassicollis, **179**

Skeleton, of turtle, **33**
Slider, **153**
Smooth Softshell Turtle, **229**
Snake-necked Turtle, **36–37**
Snapping Turtle, **123**, **143**
Spider Tortoise, **213**
Spiny Turtle, **166–167**, **169**
Spotted Turtle, **109**, **155**
Starred Tortoise, **199**
Sternotherus depressus, **186**
Sternotherus odoratus, **191**
Stinkpot, **191**
Striped Mud Turtle, **187**
Suwannee River Turtle, **30**
Terrapene carolina, **112**, **113**, **114–115**
Terrapene carolina carolina, **35**
Terrapene ornata ornata, **183**
Terrapene sp., **181**
Terrpene carolina triunguis, **182**
Testudo graeca, **214–215**, **217**
Testudo hermanni, **23**, **219**
Three-toed Box Turtle, **182**
Trionyx mutica, **229**
Trionyx triunguis, **228**
Twist-necked Turtle, **240**
Wood Turtle, **20**, **89**, **156**, **157**
Yellow Mud Turtle, **189**
Yellow-bellied Mud Turtle, **244**
Yellow-footed Tortoise, **126–127**
Yellow-legged Tortoise, **196**
Yellow-spotted River Turtle, **248**, **249**